The Bafaw Language (Bantu A10)

The Bafaw Language (Bantu A10)

Edited by
Emmanuel N. Chia
Vincent A. Tanda
Ayu'nwi N. Neba

Langaa Research & Publishing CIG
Mankon, Bamenda

Publisher:
Langaa RPCIG
Langaa Research & Publishing Common Initiative Group
P.O. Box 902 Mankon
Bamenda
North West Region
Cameroon
Langaagrp@gmail.com
www.langaa-rpcig.net

Distributed outside N. America by African Books Collective
orders@africanbookscollective.com
www.africanbookscollective.com

Distributed in N. America by Michigan State University Press
msupress@msu.edu
www.msupress.msu.edu

ISBN: 9956-578-69-X

© Emmanel N. Chia, Vincent A. Tanda
& Ayu'nwi N. Neba   2011

DISCLAIMER

All views expressed in this publication are those of the author and do not necessarily reflect the views of Langaa RPCIG.

Content

List of Contributors vii
Foreword ix

Chapter One
The Bafaw Language: A Sociolinguistic Survey
Emmanuel N. Chia 1

Chapter Two
Aspects of the Phonology of Bafaw
Ayu'nwi N. Neba 17

Chapter Three
The Noun Class System of Bafaw
Lydia E Ebah, Ayu'nwi N. Neba and Emmanuel N. Chia 39

Chapter Four
The Verb Morphology of Bafaw
Michael E. Apuge, and Ayu'nwi N. Neba 65

Chapter Five
The Syntax of Nfaw
Vincent A. Ambe 89

Chapter Six
Towards the Development of a Functional Bafaw
   Literacy Programme
Blasius Agha-ah Chiatoh 125

Chapter Seven
A Review of Nfaw Orthography: Some Proposals
Ayu'nwi N. Neba 145

Chapter Eight
Thematic Glossary of Nfaw
Emmanuel N. Tabah and Emmanuel N Chia 153

List of Contributors

Ayu'nwi N. Neba Teaches Linguistics and English Language at the University of Buea, Cameroon. Holds a PhD in Linguistics and has research interests in Tone in African Languages, and Language Education and Language Use and Phonology in General.

Blassius A. Chiatoh Holds a PhD in Applied Linguistics and Mother Tongue Education. He was formerly a field researcher at the Centre for Applied Linguistics in Yaounde. He currently lectures at the Department of Linguistics at the University of Buea. He has published widely in various scientific journals both national and international.

Emmanuel N. Chia Is Professor of Linguistics, former Deputy Vice Chancellor of Internal control and Evaluation; Former Deputy Vice Chancellor in charge of Research and cooperation and Currently Director of the Advanced School of Translators and Interpreters (ASTI) at the University of Buea.

Emmanuel N. Tabah Holds a Masters Degree in Linguistics and currently lectures in the Departments of English and Linguistics at the University of Buea.

Lydia E. Ebah Holds a Maitrise in Linguistics. She has done a lot of field work on Bafaw. She currently works at the University of Buea.

Michael E. Apuge Holds a Masters Degree in Linguistics. He is currently working towards a terminal Degree in Syntactic Theory. Former senior lecturer in the Department of Linguistics, University of Buea, he is presently Head of Department of English at the University of Maroua, Cameroon. He has research interests in Syntactic Theory.

Vincent A. Tanda Holds a PhD in Computational Linguistics and Syntactic theory and has research interests in Syntactic Theory, Applied Linguistics. He is currently Head of the Department of Linguistics at the University of Buea.

Foreword

This book entitled *The Bafaw Language (Bantu A10)* falls within the language research programme of the Department of Linguistics, Faculty of Arts, of the University of Buea. The programme was conceived to meet the need to provide grammatical descriptions of the languages within the vicinity of the university, particularly those on which no work had been carried out. Though this work could be construed as the grammar of Bafaw, it departs from the type of grammar that seeks to prove the viability of a new paradigm. Being the first serious piece of work on this language, the work aims to account generally for the data of Bafaw, thus laying the foundation for more advanced work in the future. The urgency of this project was further heightened by the threat of endangerment that looms over most Cameroonian indigenous languages. Since charity begins at home, the programme started with the description of Mokpe, the language of the natives of Buea, from where work would then progress outwards into the hinterland. This work would, from the perspective of our department, also satisfy the outreach mission of the university, to visibly impact on the development of the nation since for linguists, the development of people begins with their language and culture so as to lay a solid foundation for indigenous literacy, basis for any meaningful future development.

A sketch grammar of a language should provide a description of at least the three basic levels of language study. These comprise: the phonology, i.e. the sound system; the morphology (or lexis) of the language and thirdly, the syntax. A glance at the organisation of this work, especially chapters 2, 3, 4 and 5, provides evidence not only that this requirement has been met but that the work goes far beyond to provide a sociolinguistic survey of the Bafaw language community at the introductory chapter and three other chapters, 6, 7 and 8, respectively of a discussion of the development of functional literacy in Bafaw, a review of the Bafaw orthography and a thematic glossary of the language.

Put differently, chapter one situates the language geographically and genetically, traces the interesting migration history of Bafaw from its cradle to its present situation of dispersion into several villages. Their interaction with friends and foes, in time of peace as in time of war along their migratory path, is painstakingly documented. All told, their neighbours through time have impacted negatively on the Bafaw people, on their land, language and culture bringing them to the brinks of extinction as evidenced by the paucity of their children in the schools within and around their community. Suggestions are made to rescue the situation as a matter of urgency. Chapter two studies the sound system at both the phonetic and phonemic levels and establishes an inventory of distinctive sounds thus, laying the groundwork for the provision of an orthography. Phonological processes have been discussed, rules formulated and an inventory of tones done, all this, guided by foundational theories of classical phonemics.

The morphology of the language is studied in chapters three and four. Chapter three describes the noun class system of Bafaw strictly following earlier classifications of Bantu languages by Guthrie (1948:11) and Meeussen (1967) and comes out with 13 noun classes. One of the interesting findings of this investigation is that to identify the prefixes of different classes, one must appeal to the phonology of the language. A number of concords have been discussed and presented. Chapter four studies the verb morphology beginning with verb classes to identify the various verbal elements of the language and to determine their distribution and functions. Thus, this chapter successively examines the verb structure, tense, aspect and mood to end up with verbal extensions.

After the morphology, chapter five focuses on the combinatorial possibilities of the lexical items studied in chapters three and four to form larger constituents in Bafaw language. It begins with a study of word categories and successively proceeds to basic word order, noun phrases, focus, interrogative and imperative constructions in all their ramifications. However, the most detailed descriptions deal with interrogation and negation.

Chapter six attempts the establishment of a literacy programme for the Bafaw language community from the hind sight of a rich and variegated experience in the field. Recalling to mind an earlier failed initiative, which is carefully diagnosed, steps are suggested for setting up a functional and dynamic literacy programme and lessons are proffered which, heeded, should pave the way for success in the future.

Chapter seven is a reflection leading to the revision of the earlier version of the Bafaw orthography. Based on the writing habits of the native speakers (as influenced by the English writing tradition) and the principles enshrined in the General Alphabet of Cameroon Languages, two proposals are presented: (a) a 23 letter alphabet devoid of diagraphs and (b) a 27 letter alphabet including diagraphs. The choice of either will depend on the success in practical experimentation with both of them.

Generally, after an orthography has been provided for a language and mass literacy programmes are set in motion, there would be need for specialized terms for use in specific domains or fields in order to facilitate the communication of new knowledge. Chapter eight is an attempt at the development of just this kind of basic specialized vocabulary -- the thematic glossary of Bafaw language. Here, the thematic glossary is presented for only the fields of agriculture, health care delivery and religion. The principal aim therefore is to demonstrate the possibilities available to the Nfaw language committee for lexical expansion. Mechanisms developed in the field are presented, some, with clear examples to follow as need will arise. There is no intension to be exhaustive here. Yet, the importance of this exercise cannot be over-emphasized given the link between technical specialized knowledge and national development.

While making this volume a gift to the Bafaw people, it is our earnest hope that it will provide a useful resource for the Bafaw language development and an inspiration for further research and scholarship so that the dynamic stimulated by this endeavour should continue into other areas unabated.

Emmanuel Chia

Chapter One
The Bafaw Language: A Sociolingistic Survey[1]

Emmanuel N. Chia

1.0 Introduction

The Bafaw language referred to variously as the Nho, Nfaw, Nfo, Bafo, Bafowu, Afo, and Lefo (Dieu et Renaud 1983, Grimes 2000) is one of the minority coastal Bantu languages of Cameroon. Spoken by people of the same name, it is found principally in the Meme division of the South West Province. It is (as we demonstrate later) highly endangered which is one of the main motivations for this study. In the pages that follow, we will beam our searchlight, first of all, on the people who speak this language (their origin, settlement history, their socio-cultural activities, their population and their neighbours). Then we will turn next to the language situation (the dialectal distribution of the varieties of Bafaw and the genetic relationship of this language to the coastal languages). Finally, we will examine its status of endangerment and brainstorm on what rescue measures could be undertaken to avert an unpleasant situation.

1.1 Background
1.1.1 The Bafaw People
The Bafaws in their history are a reliable, hard working, proud and yet friendly, generous and royal people with a long and covetous pedigree. Their generosity throughout time has drawn in friends from all over but friends who, according to insider opinion, always overwhelmed them.

1.2 Their Origin
Personal communication from Professor Lovette Elango, a historian and native speaker, reveals that the Bafaws would have hailed from a location called Mwekan, bordering on the

Mbo plain, an infertile and barren area. Following the admonition of their ancestors to move in a South Westerly direction so as to meet with *"Mibungu"* (albinos or whitemen), most probably the Germans, who would provide them with clothes, gun powder, salt, wines, and whiskies in abundance, etc, they then set out in the direction of the sunset. Mwekan according to this source is certainly the place of origin, the cradle and point of dispersal of the Bafaw peoples (cf map 1). Dunda's (1922) report simply states that the Nfaws formerly inhabited the country to the East and North East of Kokobuma.

1.3 Settlement History
Their first port of call after leaving Mwekan was in Bakossiland where they sojourned for some time, founding a number of settlements around Nyandong. One of the biggest of the villages they founded there, Elung, according to Professor Elango, now goes by the name of Elung-Ninong. There, they had peaceful and friendly rapports (marked by intermarriages) with the Bakossi people until they clashed over fishing rights on the Mungo River. Njume (2000:9) adds that they also clashed over land and women. So they fought a fierce battle with the Bakossi people in the area now known as Kurume village.

MAP 1: NGOE'S DESCENDANTS: MIGRATION FROM CRADLE

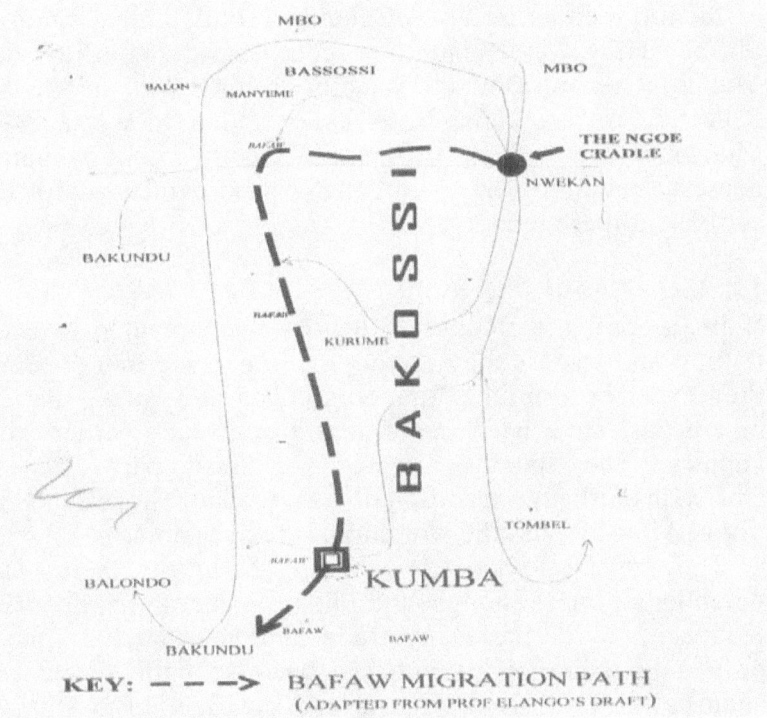

KEY: - - -> BAFAW MIGRATION PATH
(ADAPTED FROM PROF ELANGO'S DRAFT)

As they continued their southward movement along the Meme river basin which turns into Ndian river basin, they founded villages, the most important of which is Kumba town the present capital of Meme division. It remains the biggest and therefore the main settlement of the Bafaws till today although it continues to suffer a high rate of attrition as the native population cede their holdings in town to aggressive businessmen and then relocate further inland.

Beyond Kumba, their southward drive in quest of the Germans was checked by the Ekombe war (Njume 2000:9) and so they halted at Dieka and Njanga, their present south most villages. However, their traders moved into the Ndian river valley which was a major centre of commerce then, considering that this river emptied into the Rio-del-Rei, an active and famous slave trade route in the 19th century. Some of them traded as far as to Calabar. From Kumba, again some of the Bafaws extended their commercial activities via the Mungo River to Douala, a major trading area in the Wouri River. Some are thought to have settled in a place called Mundame from where they could easily access Douala, the nearest economic centre. But there is no evidence of a Bafaw settlement there today.

1.4 Socio-Cultural Activities

If in the past the Bafaws in history were reputed to excel in fishing and trade, today as they have become more sedentary, they excel in farming, producing cocoa and coffee that in the recent past have been major foreign currency earners for the country. The Bafaws are for the most part (Protestant) Christians although traditionally, they also believe in "Obasi", divine kingship and the worship of the ancestors.

They have intermarried generally both with their southern neighbours, the Balongs and their northern neighbours, the Kenyangs. With the many trade and intermarrital links, not only with their neighboring kin but also with distant people such as the Ibos from Nigeria and the Bamelikes from West Cameroon, the Bafaws and their language have experienced a lot of pressures that have had such a heavy toll on the native population and their idiom that today, "Bafaw stands in need of redefinition" (personal statement from Prof. Elango).

1.5 The Villages and Population of Bafaw

1.5.1 The Village Distribution

Many of the informants contacted listed 9 villages that comprise the Bafaw nation. However, Professor Elango added another one which he called Ngolobolo. According to him this is one of the original Bafaw villages which, because of the extraordinarily generous nature of the Bafaw person, is now inhabited entirely by non-natives. This further explains the irony of the geniality of the Bafaws: being so welcoming as to be always overwhelmed. This said, the Bafaw villages running from north to south along the Meme river basin are the following:

1. Kokobuma (also called Ekobum)
2. Kombone
3. Ngolobolo
4. Dikome
5. Kurume
6. Ikiliwindi (Kindi)
7. Mambanda (Mamban)
8. Kumba Town
9. Dieka
10. Njanga

The first six villages are situated along the Kumba-Mamfe road in Konye Subdivision; 7 and 8 are within Kumba Central while 9 and 10 are further south, precisely in Mbonge Subdivision (see map2).

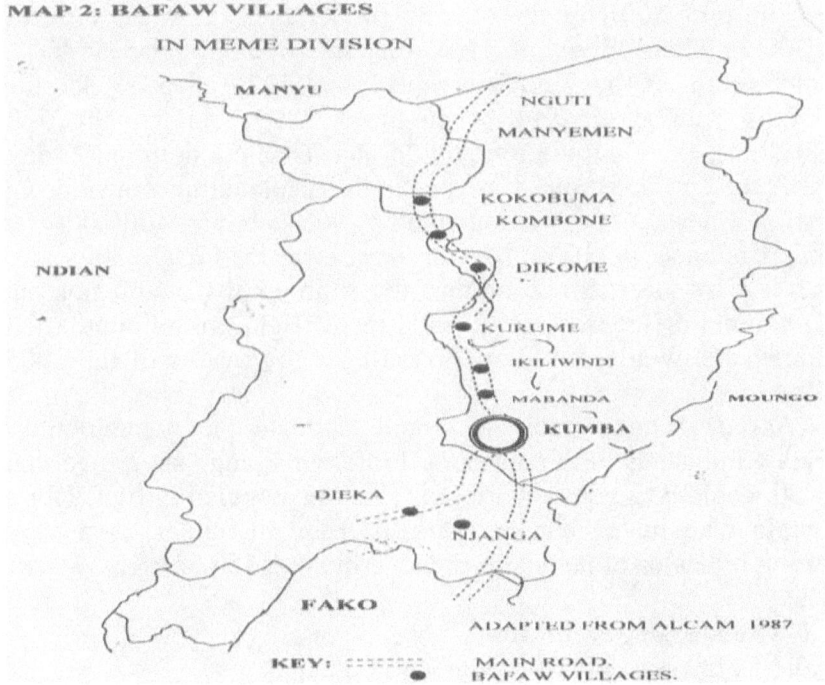

1.5.2 The population riddle

Grimes (2000) lumps up the Bafaws with the Balongs, probably from field estimates available at the Societe Internationale de Linguistique (S.I.L Yaounde 1980) to give a total population figure of 8,400 inhabitants, a figure that places both languages at high risk of endangerment as we shall see later. Because of this mix-up, pretty recurrent in developing countries as a result of the absence of reliable census figures, we are unable to come up with verifiable population statistics for the Bafaw people.

However, during the field trip, an informant estimated that the population of the Bafaws in their largest village, Kumba Town, would not exceed 700 and that the native population of the rest of the villages would not count more than 100 each. Following this logic, one could estimate the total population to be 700 plus 800 (for the other eight villages) giving a total of 1,500 in Meme division. However, this does not appear to be convincing. If by Dunda's report in 1922 (cf page 4), the Bafaws numbered 2,448 (770 males, 895 females and 783 children), their population should at least have doubled eighty years after. This would be particularly plausible considering that Cameroon population which was about 5,000,000 at independence in 1960 has sky-rocketed to 17,000,000 only forty years after. Since neither the Municipal Council nor the Divisional office in Kumba could throw light on the population riddle, one would only have to wait for the results of the 2005 census.

Asked at how much he would estimate the population of Bafaw indigenes in the diaspora, Professor Elango suggested that 1000 would be a generous figure. This low population figure for a people who have been pressurized from all angles, is a very strong indicator of language endangerment and its worries.

1.6 The language situation

1.6.1 Bafaw and its neighbouring languages

On account of the close ties that the Bafaws have had all along with their neighbours, their language has recorded extensive lexical borrowings from them, particularly Akoose, Balong,

Efik, Kenyang and Cameroon Pidgin English. It is probably for this reason that some researchers have tended to consider Bafaw and Balong as dialects of the same language. However, the Linguistic Atlas of Cameroon (ALCAM 1983) identifies Bafaw (Nho) as clearly separate, coding it as 641 as distinct from Balong 642, Akoose 652 and Oroko 632.

1.6.2 The Dialect Situation

Although ALCAM maintains that Bafaw does not exhibit any strong regional dialectal variation, the native speakers recognize three separate social varieties of the language. The people from around Kokobuma down to Dikome use a variety commonly referred to as Litom. From Kurume down to Kumba town, they identify another variety, Lefo, while further south of Kumba, a third variety spoken by the people of Njanga and Dieka obtains. While native speakers easily point to Litom as the original dialect because of its relative "purity" (i.e. it is least adulterated), the main variety remains Lefo by virtue of the size and dynamism of its population of speakers. These varieties are of course mutually intelligible but differ in prestige and accent so that the native speakers are able to identify themselves as belonging to one or the other on the basis of their speech characteristics.

However, despite the social, temporal and spatial distances that have separated the Bafaws from the Bakossis, the Bassossis and the Balongs, they all unanimously claim to be descendants of a common ancestor, Ngoe, and to be close relatives of the brotherly people of Oroko.

1.6.3 Bafaw and its Genetic Classification

According to Guthrie's (1971) classification of the Bantu languages of Western Equatorial Guinea, Bafaw falls under Zone A15. However, in the more recent ALCAM classification of the Coastal Bantu languages using lexicostatistical methods, morphological and syntactic data, Bafaw falls under Zone 6 which includes Guthrie's zones A10 – A20 – A30.

Bafaw and its sister coastal Bantu languages, indicated in clusters at the bottom of the following chart, fall under the Niger-Kordofanian phylum with the related details given.

Chart 1: Language family from which Bafaw derives.

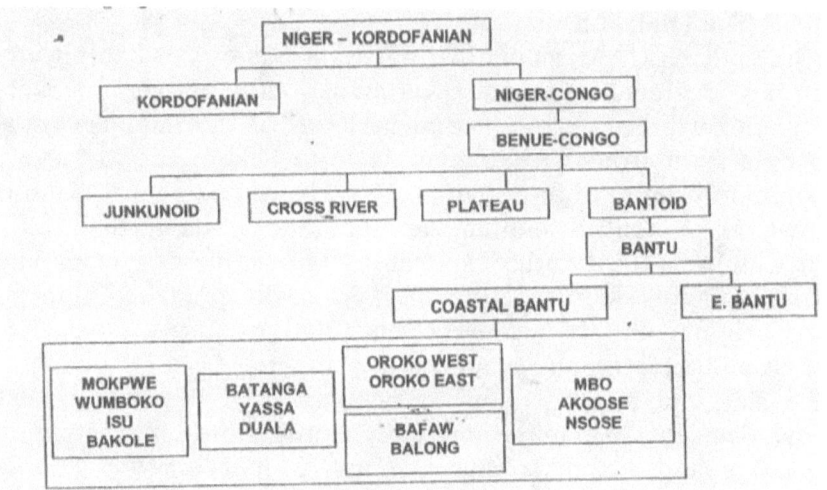

1.7 The Bafaw Language Endangered?
The metaphor of language endangerment (cf Chia 2006:115) is used to describe the threat to the continued existence of a language when it faces a combination of pressures likely to result in the non-use of it (its death) for, as Shakespeare eloquently puts it in Macbeth, "if you look into the seeds of time…..(you can) say which grain will grow and which will not….". Some of these pressures or contexts in which they are exerted are discussed here.

1.7.1 Bafaw Speaking Children and School Attendance
One pertinent area in which the status of endangerment of Bafaw language could be monitored was school attendance. The working hypothesis was that if schools in the native area of this language

registered a sizeable population of Bafaw speaking primary school children, then there would be no cause for alarm with respect to the future of the language. To verify this hypothesis, we constructed and administered a questionnaire to classes one and seven of four schools selected uniquely on the basis of their nearness to the Bafaw language native community. The schools were the following: Government Practising School (GPS), Kumba Town, situated near the central market; Presbyterian Primary School (PPS) situated in the heart of the main native village and next door to the palace of the Paramount Fon of the Bafaw people; Cameroon Baptist Convention Primary School (CBS) situated in Meta Quarter and next door to the village in question and finally, Mabanda Government School (MGS), the only school in Mabanda, the second village sampled. One of the key questions asked was how many Bafaw speaking children there were in the class. In each class, they stepped out and were counted (male and female) by the class teacher. The following table provides the statistics obtained.

Table 1: School attendance of Bafaw speaking children

Classes Sample D	Bafaw Males	Bafaw Females	Sub Total	Class Total	%
GPS 1	2	0	2	60	3.3
GPS VII	0	0	0	88	0
PPS 1	1	5	6	35	17.1
PPS VII	3	1	4	55	7.2
CBS 1	1	1	2	30	6.6
CBS VII	2	1	3	48	6.2
MGS 1	4	6	10	27	37
MGS VII	5	2	7	27	25.9
TOTAL	18	16	34	370	9.1

From the above data we notice that the highest number of Bafaw children recorded in any single school was 17 (in Mabanda, i.e. MGS I and MGS VII), almost as high as all the other schools put together. Over all, the population of Bafaw children in these schools is not very encouraging. We were reliably informed that school attendance in the other villages away from Kumba was not much different. With respect to gender, the distribution for the Bafaw children sampled stands as follows: 18 male, 16 female. There are usually more children in class one than in class seven which suggests a 30% drop out rate along the way. Also, the average percentage score of Bafaw children in the data, 34 on 370 which is 9.1 is pretty low. The probability of obtaining a sizeable Bafaw population from the classes chosen using simple random sampling (that is, picking every nth child) would even have been worse. Also, although identified as Bafaw speaking children, the proficiency of the few we got in the language could not be ascertained. They claimed to be able to speak the language but how much of the language they could actually speak was not tested. In the classroom situation in which it was forbidden to use the vernacular, all of them were struggling to learn English (and some French), but all of them were fluent speakers of Cameroon Pidgin English (CPE) which they spoke almost everywhere except in class (personal information from the class teachers). This confirms the findings of Mbangwana (1983) according to which, 97% of children sampled in Kumba were reported to use CPE outside the home. In our present survey, most of the teachers (including Ibos) were foreign to the Bafaw language.

1.7.2 Other Indices of the Bafaw Language Endangerment
From the foregoing, it seems evident that a number of historical and social pressures have conspired to endanger the continued existence of the Bafaw language and these include inter alia the following:

The many wars that the Bafaws fought in their southward drive toward the Atlantic Ocean must have drastically decimated their native population.

The inviting nature of the embattled people of Bafaw, resulting in intermarriages and occupation of their land has, paradoxically, not worked in their favour. Intermarriage in most contexts means the language of the home is something other than the mother tongue of either spouse. Perhaps also as a consequence of the foregoing, Bafaw speakers do not appear at a level of statistical significance to be counted as one of the speech forms in Kumba Central. The Sociolinguistic survey of urban centers in Cameroon (Koenig, Chia and Povey, 1983:40) is in reference.

Neighbouring languages have impinged negatively on Bafaw leaving a high index of borrowings and interferences. The borrowings that one might frown at are the esthetic type (involving the introduction of foreign items because they sound "better" or pedantic) to replace existing native expressions. This can set off a chain of undesirable changes in the language that may finally impoverish the content and structure of the native idiom.

The language is not codified and is therefore far from being introduced into the formal school system as have some other indigenous languages of Cameroon.

The population of Bafaw speaking children in the schools of their major native villages (Kumba and Mabanda), at an age where enrollment in school is mandatory, is disquietingly low.

There is apparent lack of allegiance to the language as evidenced by bitter quarrels and concomitant sloth to pursue the projected development and codification of the Bafaw native idiom.

The use of Duala or CPE in the churches of their native villages instead of Bafaw, is not a good omen for the future of Bafaw as this ineluctably prepares the way for a situation of language shift.

Most adult natives are trilingual in Bafaw, CPE and Duala while those who have schooled up to and beyond secondary school have added English and some French (the two official languages of the Republic) to their linguistic baggage. Since every one speaks CPE in the remotest of Bafaw villages, this language may already be undergoing the process of language shift hinted above, shifting perhaps to the all pervasive Cameron Pidgin English.

The above indices confirm Nettle and Suzanne Romaine's conclusion cited in Okwudishu (2006:129), that

> If you look in detail why languages are dying out, it is because there are real pressures on people that are not democratic and not very progressive. Perhaps their land is being taken away from them. Perhaps their environment is being destroyed; so, language can be a marker of something more profound or something troubling that's going on.

In view of the foregoing it can be said without much fear of an error, and until more reliable census figures say the contrary, that the Bafaw language is at "high risk of extinction" following the 2002 classification of endangered languages published in Chia (2006:123) cited earlier. The next question is why worry since for others, extinction would constitute a reduction of the language burden for the country?

1.7.3 Why Bother?
Generally, linguists and other well meaning scholars worry about language loss because a language is primarily an identity, an asset, a resource and a tool not only of communication to its native speakers but also a means for analyzing and synthesizing the world (Crawford 1995:33). Each language is a custodian and an expression of the culture (knowledge and values) of the members of its speech community. Linguistic categories such as number, gender, case, tense, aspect and many others are not so much discovered in experience as it is the case that they are imposed on it by language. To lose such a tool is to lose a way of constructing reality, a perspective evolved over many generations. To buttress this argument, Crawford cites the following Darwinian analogy:

Evolutionary biologists recognize the great advantage held by species that maintain the greatest possible diversity. Disasters occur when only one strain of wheat or corn, a mono-culture is planted everywhere. With no variation, there is no potential to meet changing conditions. In the development of new science concepts, a monolanguage holds the same dangers as a monoculture. Because languages partition reality differently, they offer different models of how the world works. There is absolutely no reason why the metaphors provided in English are superior to those of the other languages (Schrock, 1986).

Loss of the Bafaw language (or any other) will represent the loss of the culture, roots, sense of self worth and identity of the Bafaw peoples. It would represent a loss of intellectual diversity for Cameroon and the peoples of the world in general. In a recent study Bitjaa (2004:487) identifies 19 languages in Cameroon as extinct and 76 others in the throes of death.

1.8 What to do

A lot can be done and a lot should be done. Before going ahead to indicate what can be done, which is fairly obvious from a reading of the foregoing, it is necessary to indicate clearly that the people directly in charge are the Bafaw people themselves. They are the undisputed owners of the language. It goes without saying that the primary users of the language will be the greatest losers from its eventual extinction. It stands to reason therefore, that the people most qualified to do anything effective to halt the impending process of extinction of this language would be the elite of the Bafaw language community. Only they are capable of discerning the impact of the danger that threatens the continuous existence of their language and culture. The local illiterate farmer, young or old, male or female would be too busy wrestling with the problems of everyday survival to have time for language issues. That said, the following suggestions (among others) could be helpful in rescuing the language.

It would be necessary to jump start, or revamp the defunct Bafaw language Development Committee. This committee is also commonly referred to as the language academy. Generally, its task will be to pick up the bits and pieces of the orthography that was already underway when it was unfortunately abandoned, and then to finalize it.

The next step will be to prepare didactic materials in this language: readers, arithmetic books, dictionaries etc, and train teachers to teach Bafaw. The good news is that there are still many native speakers of the language who can take up this responsibility.

In case of need, applications could be addressed to the Department of Linguistics of the University of Buea, the Societe Internationale de Linguistique (SIL) and the National Association of Cameroon Language Committee (NACALCO) in Yaounde, for technical assistance.

Once teachers and teaching materials are ready, the language could be introduced into the schools of their native communities in Cameroon. There should no longer be fear that government, as in the past, might frown on such a venture since Law N$^{\circ}$ 98/004 of 14 April 1998 purports to promote just this kind of linguistic and cultural development.

One of the most important factors to be discussed is the funding. In all the example cases that are running well in the country today, the initial finances have been generated by the language community through the selfless sacrifices of the elite. The respective municipalities and church management have also been indirectly instrumental, but the initial funding, the organization towards publication didactic materials and training of teachers and writers generally have been the responsibility of the local and external elite of the community in question. Experience has shown that if a community decides to wait for government assistance in order to begin, it may wait forever.

The native speakers must cultivate allegiance and a positive attitude towards their culture and language: speak it among themselves and with their children in their homes; make it a language of literacy, worship and play; write correspondences, stories, literature in it and publish newspapers and books in it.

Thus, the responsibility for the resuscitation of the Bafaw language lies squarely on the shoulders of this language community itself. The initiative, ownership and management of the project must be uniquely that of the Bafaw people. Fortunately there are many inspiring examples to learn from in Cameroon, Africa and the world. It takes determination, coordination and a spirit of sacrifice because it is something worthy of every linguistic group.

1.9 Conclusion

This paper set out to profile the Bafaw language from the perspective that as one of the minority languages of Cameroon, it faces the danger of extinction. The various pressures on the language and its speakers from the cradle of its ancestor down to its present situation of segmentation into many dispersed villages were examined. The threat of extinction was shown to be imminent and conservation and renewal measures suggested to reverse the situation.

Notes

1. This paper has been possible thanks to the generous cooperation of the following personalities and elite of Bafaw in giving us their time, information and documentation: Prof Elango, Messrs, Maurice Eseme, Akwo John Eyoh, Ntem B.R., Njuh Francis, Wilson Eseme, Mukete Philemon, Mmes Ntiege, Nku F and Ida Ntube.

References

ALCAM (1983). *Atlas Linguistique du Cameroun, Inventaire Première*. ACCT, CERDOTOLA, DGRST.

Bitjaa, Kody Zachee Denis. 2004. *La Dynamique des langues Camerounaises en contact avec le frañais*. P (482 – 492) NYI Dissertation.

Carr F.B. 1923. *An Assessment Report on the Tribal Area of Balong in Kumba Division of the Cameroons Province*.

Chia, E. 2006:123."Rescuing Endangered Cameroonian Languages for National Development" in *African Linguistics and development of African communities*, CODESRIA, Dakar.

Crawford, J. 1995. Endangered Native American Languages. What is to be Done and why? *Bilingual Research Journal* vol. 19 No. 1.

Dieu, M. and P. Renaud, 1983.*Linguistic Atlas of Cameroon*. Paris: ACCT.

Dunda R.W.M.1922. *Bafaw Assessment Report*. (Seventy page report by the District Officer of Kumba dated 16/12/22)

Ebah, L. 1990. *The Noun Class System of Bafaw*. A Maitrise Project, University of Yaounde.

Grimes, Babara and Grimes, Joseph, E., eds. 2000. *Ethnologue*, Vol.1: Languages of the World, Dallas, Texas: SIL.

Gutherie, M., 1971 *Contributions from Comparative Bantu Studies to the Pre-History of Africa*, Dalby D, New York.

Koenig, Chia and Povey. 1983. The Sociolinguistic Survey of Urban Centers in Cameroon. Crossroads Press, California.

Mbangwana, N. Paul (1983: 88) "The Scope and role of Pidgin English in Cameroon" in *A Sociolinguistic Profile of Urban Centers in Cameroon*. Crossroads Press California.

Njume, C S. (2000) *On wh- operations in Nfaw*. UB Long Essay.

Okwudishu (2006) "Of the Tongue – Tied and Vanishing Voices: Implications for African Development" in *African Linguistics and the development of African Communities pp 129 – 139*.

Chapter Two
Aspects of the Phonology of Bafaw

Ayu'nwi N. Neba

2.0 Introduction
As mentioned in the introduction of this book, Bafaw has not enjoyed a lot of linguistic attention given the hurdles described in chapter six. However, some effort has been made in describing certain aspects of the language. Ebah (1988) for example in a Maîtrise project did a brief description of the noun class system of the language. Njume (2002) for a B.A. Long Essay analysed Wh-Operators. Very little has been done on the phonology of the language. This explains why in this chapter, we discuss the essentials of the phonology of the language. We believe that an in-depth analysis of the phonology of the language will go a long way to strengthen and reinforce the work already initiated in the area of orthography design and the preparation of a dictionary for the language.

2.1 The Sound System
The sounds of the language will be presented here at two levels: phonetic and then phonemic.

2.1.1 Phonetic Sounds
Chart 1 below contains the phonetic consonants while chart 2 contains the phonetic vowel sounds that we gleaned from the data that we collected for this research.

Chart 1: Phonetic Consonants

Place of Art. / Manner of Art	Bilabial	Labio-velar	Alveolar	Alv. palatal	Palatal	Velars	Labio-velar	Glottal
Stops	p b pʲ bʲ		t d tʲ dʲ			k kʲ	kp g b	ʔ
	m		n		ɲ	ŋ	ŋw	
	m̥		n̥			ŋ̊		
Fricatives	β	f	s	ʃ				
Affricates		bv		dʒ		kf gv		
Approximants			l		j		w	
Prenasals	ᵐp ᵐb		ⁿt ⁿd			ᵑk ᵑg		
Implosives	ɓ							

These consonant sounds are illustrated in the data below.

1.

p	píndípíndí	'charcoal'	b	bùwèŋ		'tree'
	ɛpèŋ	'thigh'		m̀bɔ̀lɔ̀		'pestle'
t	ɛtú	'shoulder'	d	ǹdúlù		'sun'
	ǹtúm	'stick'		dìlɛ́		'stone'
k	kém	'monkey'	kʲ	ɛkʲìʔ		'iron'
	bìdʒúkà	'pits'		lìsákʲɪ		'dance'
kp	ɛkpútú	'cap'	gb	m̀gbáŋgálá		'tray/plate'
	ɛkpà	'bag'		lìgbɛ		'liver'
ʔ	nèkɔʔ	'plantain'	m	màdíʔ		'water'
	lìkóʔ	'cloud'		ɛjêm̀		'tongue'

n	lìfìn	'forest'	ɲ	ɲó	'snake'	
	ǹtúm̀	'stick'		ɲùɲ	'hair'	
ŋ	bìdùŋ	'baskets'	m̪	m̀bɔ̆	'pot'	
	ŋkùm	'tails'		m̀bɔ̀lɔ̀	'pestle'	
ṇ	ǹlùŋá	'bucket'	ŋ̀	ŋ̀gulí	'belt'	
	ǹdă	'house'		ŋ̀gùʃú	'mat'	
f	ɛfʲăŋ	'broom'	bv	ŋ̀kŭmbvé	'blanket'	
	lìfíɲ	'forest'		ǹláàmbvé	'branch'	
ʃ	ŋ̀gùʃú	'mat'	s	ɛ̀pɛ̀síŋkù	'blanket'	
	ɛ̀ʃùkúlù	'school'		sɔ̆	'thatch'	
dʒ	dʒáŋgòlò	'mango'	kf	kfʷɛ́ʔ	'snail'	
	dʒídʒàŋ	'pineapple'		ɛ̀kfùʔ	'bowl/mortar'	
gv	ŋ̀gvì	'corn'	l	lìbàʔ	'cloth/dress'	
				ɛ̀kfuʔ	'mortar'	
j	jâɲi	'buy'	w	wùdû	'night'	
	ɛ̀jáɓ	'tall'		ŋ̀gàwè	'cow/animal'	
ᵐb	ɛ̀kàᵐbìkáᵐbì	'lizard'	ᵑg	m̀gbáŋgálá	'tray/plate'	
				ᵑgààᵑgù	'umbrella'	
ⁿd	m̀bíⁿdâ	'crab'	ɓ	ɓɔ̀	'they'	
	lìlénd̚	'knife'				
β	βá:luʔ	'canoe'	pʲ	píndípíndí	'charcoal'	
dʲ			bʲ	bʲìfáʔ	'dandruff'	
	lìdʲă	'food'		ɛ̀jábʲé	'tall'	
	dʲímí	'seal'				
tʲ	tʲítʲíʔ	'star'	ŋʷ	àŋʷá̋	'cat'	
				ŋʷáŋ	'drink'	

Table 2 Phonetic Vowel Sounds

```
    i   i:         ɨ           u   u:
      ɪ
    e   e:         ə         o   o:
      ɛ   ɛ:                 ɔ   ɔ:
              a   ã   a:
```

These sounds are illustrated in the following words.
2.

i	lìbà	'cloth'	i:	màkǐ:	'blood'
	lìléndá	'knife'		ŋʷǐ:	'pigs'
u	ǹdúlù	'sun'	ɪ	màdí?	'water'
	mákún	'beans'		dʷí	'toilet'
ɨ	m̀bɨ̌	'valley'	u:	dù:	'night'
	nɨ̀ɲí	'love'		ǹlù:ŋgá	'basket'
e:	né:bʷà	'spider'	ɛ	ɛ̀pɛ̀ŋ	'teeth'
				ɛ̀ké	'arm'
ə	ŋ̀kfùmé	'sub chief'	e	dìléndé	'knife'
	ɛ̀pə̀ŋ	'teeth/thigh'			
ɛ:	pɛ̀:	'cutlass'	o:	m̀bò:	'lake/sea'
	ǹlɛ́:	'uncle'			
ɔ	mɔ̀	'his/man'	ɔ:	ʃɔ́:wá	'thatch'
	pɔ̀ŋ	'tell'		ŋ̀gɔ̀:lì	'voice'
o	lòᵑgé	'life'	ã:	ŋʷãŋ	'drink'
	ɛ̀bòwà	'prison'		àŋʷã́	' cat'
a:	βà:lù?	'canoe'	a	dʲíjá	'eat'
	ɛ̀bá:mí	'quarrel'		ʃɔ́:wá	'thatch'

The sounds presented above are attested at the phonetic level. These sounds are not all contrastive in this language. In the next section, we consider the phonemic status of these sounds.

2.2 Phonemic Status of Sounds
2.2.1 Brief Comments
Before we embark on establishing the phonemic status of the sounds presented in 2.2.1, a number of comments are in order here.

The prenasalized consonants [mb], [nt], [nd], and [ŋk] etc only occur word medially in the language. At word initial position, the initial nasal is always syllabic; that is, it is the nucleus of a syllable. On the other hand, [g] does not exist in this language. Every time it occurs, it is always preceded by [ŋ]. This suggests that in such a situation, [ŋg] constitutes a single prenasalised consonant. This poses serious problems for symmetry. Why would [ŋg] alone pattern differently? It is not evident why this should be the case. It is important to note that [ŋ] occurs only at word final position without a velar oral sound after it. This means that its occurrence is highly predictable. The question that arises is that when the sequence [ŋg] appears word initially when the noun in which it occurs is supposed to take a syllabic nasal as a nominal prefix, does the [ŋ] automatically become syllabic or does the nominal prefix still attach to the noun creating a –NN- sequence? We return to this discussion in some detail below. The implosive [ɓ] is highly limited in occurrence. Out of a word list of about 5000 words, the sound features only in two words. This is also true of the bilabial fricative [β] and the affricate [gv] which was found to occur only in one word [ŋ̀gvì] 'corn'. This limitation in the occurrence of these sounds could be suggesting that they are either not phonemic in the language or are phasing out in the process of language change. This is an issue which deserves more investigation.

The sounds [ʒ], [z] and [v] are not attested in the language despite the fact that their voiceless counterparts [ʃ], [s], [f] respectively do exist. In contrast, we notice that to respect the principle of symmetry, the language makes use of [dʒ] evidently in place of [ʒ] and [bv] in the place of [v]. It should be pointed out that while [bv] does exist, [pf] is not attested in the language and while [dʒ] does exist, [tʃ] is absent. What is evident from these facts is that voiced fricatives seem to be marked in the language. This explains why [β] is only attested sparingly in the language-two out of five thousand words. The relationship between voiceless fricatives and their voice counterparts can be summarised as in 3 below.

3. $\begin{Bmatrix} s \\ \int \end{Bmatrix}$ [dʒ]

  [f]   [bv]

The implication of this analysis is that if voiceless fricatives become their voice counterparts, then the voiceless fricatives in (3) will change to the voiced affricatives as indicated.

As far as vowels are concerned, long vowels are limited in occurrence although there is enough evidence that they are contrastive in the language. Only the low central vowel in the language has a nasalized counterpart and this is predictable as we will demonstrate below. The fact that nasalization should be noticed uniquely with [a] is no strange phenomenon. Ferguson (1963, 1975) and Ruhlen (1978) point out that open vowels, pronounced with the tongue lowered and the jaw open, allow for a greater degree of velic opening. Nasalisation is thus easier to be produced with the more open vowels. [a] is the only open vowel attested in Bafaw and this is certainly why this vowel alone should be nasalized.

After briefly making these basic comments, we now make an attempt at establishing contrastive evidence for the phonetic sounds presented above and then move on to presenting the phonemic charts containing all the phonemes of the language.

2.2.2 Consonant Contrasts

The minimal pairs below illustrate the contrastive function of consonant sounds in Bafaw.

4.

/p/, /l/	ɛpɛŋ	'thigh'	ɛlɛŋ	'palm tree'
/j/, /w/	lìjá	'birth'	lìwá	'death'
/kp/, /k/	ɛ́ká	'lamp'	ɛ̀kpà	'bag'
/s/, /dʒ/	súm	'sell'	dʒŭm	'sew'
/n/, /ŋ/	lìbàn	'poverty'	lìbàŋ	'clouds'
/kf/, /t/	kfú	'fowl'	tú	'spoon'
/b/, /j/	lìbɔ̀ʔ	'pumpkin'	lìjɔ̀ʔ	'thorn'
/d/, /l/	lìbúʔ	'site'	dìbúʔ	'nine'
/k/, /ʃ/	ɛ̀ké	'hand'	ɛ̀ʃɛ́	'feather'
/t/, /w/	ɛ̀kú	'shoulder'	ɛ̀wú/ɛ̀gvú	'death'
/ʔ/, /n/	lìbúʔ	'site'	lìbùn	'farm house'
/ɲ/, /k/	ɲŏ	'snake'	kŏ	'grow'
/b/, /m/	bɔ́ʔ	'them'	mɔ́	'him/her'
/f/, /l/	ɛfó	'one'	ɛló	'spear/arrow'
/k/, /s/	kŏ	'grow'	sŏ	'thatch'

We could not find minimal pairs for all the suspicious pairs that the consonants in the chart above can produce. However, the frequency of occurrence of most of the sounds and their occurrence in near minimal pairs suggest that they can be considered as phonemes. These sounds are ŋk, ŋg, nd, bv, ß, gv, mb, and ɓ.

A number of the consonants presented in the chart above are not phonemic. These include the palatalised sounds pʲ, bʲ, tʲ, dʲ, and kʲ. These sounds are in complementary distribution with p, b, t, d, and k respectively. The rules that derive the allophones from their respective phonemes are discussed and presented below.

The Bafaw Language (Bantu A10)

We will postulate an archiphoneme N̦ for all the syllabic nasals which will undergo the rule of homorganic nasal assimilation (HNA) to yield m̀, ǹ, and ŋ̀. This archiphoneme will also be used as part of prenasalised sounds. With this, the Bafaw consonant phonemic chart is presented below.

Place of Art / Manner of Art	Bilabial	Labio-velar	Alveolar	Alveo-palatal	Palatal	Velar	Labio-velar	Glottal
Stops	p b		t d			k	kp gb	ʔ
	m		n		ɲ	ŋ		ŋw
Fricatives		F	s	ʃ				
Affricates		bv		dʒ			kf gv	
Approximants			l		j		w	
Prenasals	ᵐp ᵐb		ⁿt ⁿd			ᵑk ᵑg		
Implosive	ɓ							

2.2.3 Vowel Phonemes

As far as vowels are concerned, what is clear is that the nasalized vowel ã is in complementary distribution with a. the nasalized vowel occurs only when preceded by the velar nasal ŋʷ. For this reason, it is excluded from the vowel phonemic chart.

Long vowels are limited in occurrence in the language. We have not found minimal pairs or near minimal pairs to prove that these sounds are really contrastive. Some of these vowels especially ɛ: are produced when they are contiguous with another vowel. We assume here that a process of vowel deletion followed by compensatory lengthening should account for the surface realisation of these long vowels. We ipso facto exclude long vowels from the vowel phonemic chart. The phonological processes which account for the derivation of these sounds are stated in section 1.2.4.

In the data in 5, we attempt to show how these vowels play a contrastive function. In most of these situations we do not find minimal pairs. Consequently, we have therefore resorted to near minimal pairs to establish these phonemic contrasts.

Vowel Phonemic Contrast
5.

/ɔ/	lìbɔ̀?	'pumpkin'	/i/	ɲì	'louse'	/u/	èjúm	'dry season'
/u/	lìbù?	'place'	/ɔ/	ɲɔ̀	'snake'	/ə/	èjə́m	'tongue'
/i/	dìbù	'nine'	/a/	wá	'die'	/ɪ/	èkɪ̀	'hand'
/i/	dìbó	'Dibo'	/u/	wŭ	'wash'	/a/	èkàn	'local lamp'

Chart 4 shows the phonemic vowels attested in Bafaw.

Chart 4: Bafaw Phonemic vowel Sounds

```
    i           ɨ           u
     ɪ
      e         ə           o
       ɛ                   ɔ
              a
```

2.2.4 Phonological Processes
We mentioned in 2.2.2 and 2.2.3 that there are a number of sounds that are attested in the phonetic charts but which are eliminated from the phonemic charts because they are in complementary distribution with some other sounds. This section of the work is dedicated to the treatment of some of the processes that derive these phonetic sounds from their phonemic counterparts.

2.2.4.1 Palatalization
This is a process where a consonant is produced with an additional tongue raising towards the palatal region. Phonetically, palatalized sounds in this language are produced with some fricative effect probably because of the narrowing of the space between the tongue and the palate. Remember that [i] is a closed

vowel and when a consonant sound comes before it, this results in its palatalization. Consider the data in 6 below.

6. Phonemic Form   **Phonetic Form**
/bìkfî/   [bʲìkfî]   'yam'
/dìbù/   [djìbù]   'nine'
/ bìkì`/   [bìkʲì]   'irons'
/kìfŭŋ/   [kʲìfŭŋ]   'axe'

From the data in 6, it will be noticed that only plosives are palatalized. The environment of palatalization is before the high front tense vowel. As already explained above, palatalization is natural because [i] is a close vowel. The strength in the production of plosives and the tenseness of [i] results in the palatalization. This rule is postulated in 7 below.

7. $C \rightarrow C^j /$ ___ i

$$\begin{bmatrix} -syll \\ -nas \\ -cont \end{bmatrix} \rightarrow [+high] / \underline{\quad} \begin{bmatrix} +syll \\ +high \\ -back \\ +ATR \end{bmatrix}$$

The rule states that a plosive is palatalized in this language whenever it is followed by the high front tense unround vowel.

2.2.4.2 Homorganic Nasal Assimilation (HNA)
This process whereby a nasal consonant takes over or assimilates the features of a following contiguous consonant is illustrated by the following data.

8.a ǹdùkú   'farm'   b.ŋ̀kɔ́?   'rope'   c. m̀bó?   'squirrel'
    ǹdúlù   'sun'   ŋ̀gjă?   'hoe'   m̀bí?   'back'
    ǹdʒɔ̀   'elephant'   ŋwán   'child'   m̀bɛ̀?   'rib'

From the data in 8, all the nouns have initial nasals. It will be realised that in 8a, the nasal is [n] and it precedes coronal sounds. In 8b, it is [ŋ] preceding dorsal consonants and in 8c, it is [m] preceding labial sounds. It should be pointed out here that these nasals are nominal class markers (Ebah 1988 and Ebah et al, this volume). The occurrence of syllabic nasals [ǹ], [m̀], and [ŋ̀] is therefore predictable. These sounds are mutually exclusive. We can therefore consider them as morphophonemic alternations and since they are equally predictable, an archiphoneme can be postulated as the underlying form of these syllabic nasals. The rule that accounts for the surface realisation of this sound is stated in 9 below.

9. N → $\begin{Bmatrix} n \\ m \\ ŋ \end{Bmatrix}$ / ___ $\begin{Bmatrix} d \\ b \\ g \end{Bmatrix}$

$\begin{bmatrix} \text{-syll} \\ \text{+nas} \end{bmatrix}$ → $\begin{bmatrix} \text{αcor} \\ \text{βant} \end{bmatrix}$ / ___ $\begin{bmatrix} \text{αcor} \\ \text{βant} \end{bmatrix}$

The rule states that a nasal consonant assimilates the place features of a following consonant. The claim that the rule is making is that one can never find a nasal and a contiguous consonant which do not agree in place of articulation.

2.2.4.3 Vowel Nasalization

This is another assimilatory process where a vowel is produced with a velic release because it is preceded by a nasal consonant. The data in 10 illustrate this.

10.a. ɔ́ŋwã̀   'cat'   b. èlàŋgà   'palm wine'
     ŋwãn   'child'   mákítì   'market'
     ŋwãlan   'wife/woman'

In 10a, we notice that [a] is always nasalized, while it is not in 10b. In 10a, the nasalized vowel always follows [ŋw] while in 10b it occurs elsewhere. The conclusion that can be made is that [a] is nasalized because of the preceding velar [ŋw]. The data in 10b illustrate that [a] is not nasalized before and after nasals. This happens only with a particular sound [ŋw]. This is psychologically real given that [ŋw] and [a] are both produced at the back of the oral cavity.

2.2.4.4 Vowel Deletion and Vowel Devocalisation

These are phonological processes which are common in Bantu languages. They are motivated by the constraint on contiguous syllabic peaks across morphemes. While vowel deletion is a situation where an entire segment is phonetically lost, devocalisation on its part refers to a situation where only some phonetic features are lost. The data in 11 demonstrate these.

11a. wù-dúù 'night'   b. b^w-ălù 'canoe'   c. f^j-ăŋgú? 'sand'
    wù-kù 'mountain'   b^w-ə́ 'medicine'   f^j-ĕŋ 'mushroom'
    wù-tì 'bed'   b^w-ín 'today'   f^j-ɔ̀? 'wild pepper'
    wù-kà? 'fence'   b^w-ə̀ 'tree'

We notice in 11a that the nominal prefix is **wù-** (class 13- this is discussed in greater detail in chapter 4 below). In 11b, the same prefix surfaces as [b^w-]. In 11c, we have class 19 nouns. As we will notice in the next chapter, the underlying nominal prefix is **fì-**. Notice however that this morpheme surfaces in 11c as [f^j-]. The question to answer is what accounts for these alternations. Following our knowledge of Bantu morphology, we conclude that the underlying representations of the classes 13 and 19 prefixes are /wù-/ and /fì-/ respectively and that [b^w-], and [f^j-] are derived from these two underlying representations. We therefore assume that a glide formation rule applies which changes /u/, and /i/ to [w] and [j] respectively before another vowel. The question that arises is what accounts for the surface realisation of [wù] as [b^w-]? As we will demonstrate in chapter four, this involves the application of a dissimilation rule and a coalescence rule. These are elaborately discussed in section 4.2 of chapter four (see particularly example 16, 17 and 18 of chapter four).

The data in 11d and 11c demonstrate vowel deletion. The nouns are class 2 nouns and as we show in chapter four, the nominal prefix of class 2 is [**ba-**]. When collocated with a noun with initial root vowel (11e), the prefix vowel is lost. This is the case of complete vowel deletion.

11d. bà-kálá	'white people'	11e. b-à?	'persons'
bà-kə̀n	'guest'	b-àáɲà	'siblings'
bà-kwí?	'windows'	b- ăn	'children'
bà-bìndâ	'crabs'	b-àŋʷã	'cats'
bà-sún	'friends'	b-álân	'daughters'
bà-fɔ̀n	'chiefs'		

The worry at this point is that given the two processes of devocalisation and deletion, how they would apply given that the two processes have the same contexts of application. The answer is that devocalisation should be ordered before vowel deletion in a counter bleeding relation. Devocalisation will only affect [i] and [u] is v_1 position.

2.3 Tone
In this section of the work, we attempt to make an inventory of the tones that are attested in Nfaw and to illustrate with appropriate data the contrastive role that tone plays in this language.

The following tones are attested phonetically in the language.

The high tone (H) [´] is illustrated in 12a.
12a. píndípíndí   'charcoal'
    dʷí   'toilet'
    kə́m   'monkey'

The low tone (L) [ˋ] is illustrated in 12b.
12b. èlàŋgà   'palmwine'
    wùkùl   'hill'
    wùtì   'bed'

The rising tone
12c. m̀bǔ   'pot'
ǹdǎ   'house'
ɲǒ   'snake'
sǒ   'thatch'

The falling tone
12d. ʃâ   'termite'
èlâ   'spear'
ɲètê   'garden eggs'

The rising and falling tones are considered not as pure contour tones in African languages but as a combination of register tones HL or LH. In the data in 13, we illustrate the contrastive role that tone plays in this language.

13. /H/ m̀bí   'palm nut'   /L/ lìbí   'faces'
    lìbí   'faces'   lìbìn   'testicle'

    /R/ m̀bǐ   'black'   /F/ lìbî   'breast'

From The data in 13 we can observe that the tones presented above are also phonemic. Thus, the tonemes attested in this language are H, L, R and F.

2.4 The Syllable Structure of Bafaw

Dominantly, the open syllable type (a syllable that ends in a vowel) is attested in the languages. In a word list of about three hundred (300) monosyllabic words, only about seventy (70) of them were closed. Among those 70, the consonant in coda position is dominantly a nasal. Only about ten (10) of these words, end with consonants other than the glottal stop[1] and a nasal. This leads us to the conclusion that Bafaw prefers an open syllable, and if closed, a nasal consonant will be preferred in coda position. It should also be mentioned here that consonant clusters[2] are rare in this language. This implies that the dominant syllable type in Bafaw is the unmarked CV-syllable. In the data that follow, we illustrate the syllable types attested in the language.

2.4.1 The V- Syllable type
This is a syllable that is made up of the nucleus alone. The V can be a vowel or a syllabic nasal. This is illustrated in 14.

14a. è-bùŋ	'chair'	b. ǹ-dʒìb	'thief'
è-kə̀	'lamp'	ǹ-lə̀m	'heart'
è-fî	'bone'	m̀-fə̀n mpe?	'machete handle'

2.4.2 The CV-Syllable Type
This, as mentioned above, is the most recurrent syllable type attest in Bafaw. It is made up of the onset and the nucleus. The data in 15 illustrate this.

15a. tú	'spoon'	b. bì-kí-sá	'ribs'
sǒ	'thatch'		
ɲǒ	'snake'		

2.4.3 The CVC Syllable type
This is the only closed syllable type attested in the language. It is rare with the consonant in coda position highly restricted. The data in 16 illustrate this.

16a. kə̀m	'monkey'	b. túl	'tie'	c. lì-bà?	'cloth'
sa'ŋ	'father'	kɔ́?	'pound'	è-tá?	'barn'
bǎn	'children'	ǹ-dʒìb	'thief'	kà?	'antelope'

It can be concluded that there are only three syllable types in Bafaw namely V, CV and CVC.

2.4.4 The Phrase Glottal Stop
The glottal stop appears to be dominant in the speech of most native speakers at phrasal level. Generally, when a word ends in a vowel, there is a tendency for it to be pronounced with a

final glottal stop when at the end of a phrase or at prepausal level. Consider for example the data in 17.

17a. màbà?	'clothes'	b. màbàmámɔ̀?	'his clothes'
ǹlùùŋgá?	'bucket'	ǹlùùŋgámmìjɛ̀?	'my bucket'
ǹdʒǎ?	'hoe'	ǹdʒɛ̌:mɔ̀?	'my hoe'
mɘ̀kà?	'plantains'	màkɔ̀mámɔ̀?	'his plantains'

We realise that in isolation, the words end in a glottal stop. When in collocation with another word, the glottal stop is dropped at the end of these words and sent to the end of the phrase. This sound seems to be behaving like the final phrasal low tone in Bafut (Neba 1998, 2007) as illustrated in 18.

(18a) fâ 'give'
(18b) fámû 'give a child'
(18c) fámúwâ 'give the child'
(18d) fámúwámbô 'give the child to'
(18e) fámúwámbómúwâ 'give the child to the child'

As illustrated by the data in 18, the final low tone always surfaces on the final syllable of the phrase. This is just the same behaviour noticed with the glottal stop in Bafaw. Bafaw is therefore similar to (Bafut??) Arabela, Zaparoan language of Peru (Rich, 1963) in which the glottal stop only occurs contrasting with its absence at the end of breath groups as illustrated in 19.

19. (a) [taati nāsixinū] 'How did he say it ?' (uncertain)
    (b) [kɨsɘɘti hɛ̃eɣmi?] 'What is that?' (surprise)

In fact, the glottal stop in this language is only attested in this position. However, we need more investigation to conclude whether it is really a phoneme or an allophone. In this work, we consider it a phoneme given that it has been identified in many other related coastal Bantu languages. We must mention that in the speech of some speakers the final glottal stop is not consistently used. It sometimes surfaces and sometimes it does not. However, there was none of the speakers in our study who did not use it in at least one instant.

2.5 Ambiguous Segments
There are certain segments which are phonetically ambiguous. That is, it is not very clear whether they are functioning as consonants or vowels. The basic fact is that the way that they are interpreted affects the syllable structure of the words in which they occur. In Bafaw, the most common instance of this sort of ambiguity concerns high vowels and glides. In a sequence with a high vowel such as [ai], there are several possible interpretations which may be given to the [i]. This fact is illustrated by the data in 20 below.

2.5.1 The Glide-vowel Sequence
In this language, there are instances in which there is a phonetic sequence of a vowel and a high vowel sound. Consider the following data.

20a. [dwí]	b. [dúwí]	'toilet'
[ŋ̀gwì]	[ŋ̀gùwì]	'pig'
[ʃwî]	[ʃúwì]	'fish'
[lìkàù]	[lìkàwù]	'cocoyam'
[èfjâŋ]	[èfíjàŋ]	'broom'
[djûm]	[díjùm]	'ten'

The main question here is whether the words in 20 should be transcribed as 20a or as 20b. If we adopt the forms in 20a, then we will have to postulate consonant clusters for this language. However, since the dominant syllable structure of the language as mentioned earlier, is CV(C), and there are no other situations where we have consonant clusters like bl, pr, kl etc., it will be illogical to adopt the forms in 20a. For this reason, we find it justified following Burquest, (1998) to adopt the forms in 20b. This is why we have not postulated any CCV(C) syllable structure for this language. Notice that the adoption of the forms in 20b is cost free whereas the adoption of the forms in 20a will require the postulation of new syllable types.

2.5.2 The NC-Sequence

Another set of ambiguous segments in this language is the set of sounds where a consonant is collocated with a nasal as illustrated in 21.

21a. ŋg   nd   mb
  ǹlù:ŋgá?   'bucket'   wúndí 'rice'   màkpàmbà   'cassava'
  ǹgá:ŋgù   'umbrella'
  mŋgbáŋgálá   'tray'

The question is whether the NCs above should be considered as CC, that is consonant clusters or as the single sounds comprising two segments. In other words should these sounds be considered as prenasalised consonants or as consonant clusters? A number of factors must be taken into consideration in order to determine the status of these sounds. First, as we mentioned earlier, [g] does not feature anywhere else in the language except when preceded by the nasal [ŋ]. If we say that [ŋg] is a consonant cluster, then we may be tempted to syllabify [ǹlù:ŋgá?] 'bucket' for example as follows:

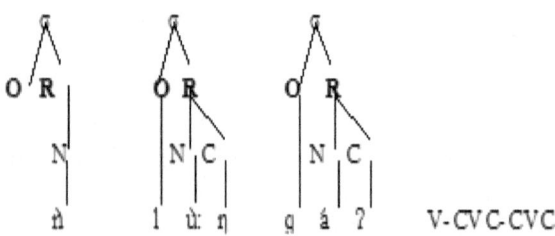

This will mean that the [g] will surface in onset position. This is a violation of a universal principle whereby the word structure is closely linked to the syllable structure as pointed out in Hyman (1975). Since [g] cannot occur in word initial position, we do not expect it to occur in onset position. Based on this and other works done on zone A narrow Bantu languages one of which is Bafaw (see Atindogbé 2002) we conclude that the NC sequences above constitute single sounds that occupy single C-slots on the skeletal tier. Recall that we do not want to postulate consonant clusters for Bafaw because of independent facts of the language.

The phonological processes treated above are just a few of the phonological processes attested in the language. An exhaustive analysis of the morphophonology of the language will obviously reveal many more processes. The few discussed here account for some of the alternations that have been encountered in this section of the work, explaining the differences between the phonemic and the phonetic sounds.

2.6 Conclusion

This chapter has examined some aspects of the phonology and morphology of Bafaw. Specifically, the sounds of the language have been identified both at the phonetic and the phonemic levels. The phonemic status of the sounds has been discussed and formulated. The inventory of tones attested in the language has been done with no tonal processes discussed, so it is not exhaustive[3].

The work done here has been guided by a foundational theory-classical phonemics which handles only foundational aspects of the phonology of languages. The morphophonology of the language has to be done and tone exhaustively analysed within a non linear and more putative tonal theory –the autosegmental phonology theory (Goldsmith (1976)). All the sounds of the language have not yet been discovered. This can only be exhaustive if the other aspects of the phonology of the language are treated as summarised by Burquest (1998):

> Phonemic analysis is an iterative process. A later stage in the analysis will frequently cause the analyst to go back to an earlier step and re-evaluate decisions made then. It should be kept in mind that all through the analysis, each decision is a hypothesis which needs to be rechecked and confirmed before it can be considered a fact Burquest (1998:39).

Notes

1. The glottal stop in coda position in this language has a special status. We discuss this later in this section.

2. There are however, some ambiguous segments in this language that make it difficult to say if they are vowels or consonants. We discuss this in detail in section 4.

3. We will like to express our gratitude to Mr Victor Mukwele and Mr Dibo Princewill for providing most of the data that we used in this chapter.

References

Atindogbe, G. G. (2002). "Accounting for Prenasals in Bantu Languages of Zone A" Occasional Papers, No 14. Communications of the Centre for Advanced Studies of African Society. Cape Town: CASAS.

Burquest, D.A. (1998) *Phonological analysis: a functional approach.* SIL Inc: U.S.A. 31-80.

Chomsky, N. and Halle, M. (1968). *The sound pattern of English.* New York: Harper and Row.

Gordon, R. G. Jr (ed) (2005). Ethnologue: Languages of the World, Fifteenth edition. Dallas, Texas: SIL International. Online version: http://www.ethnologue.com//.

Ebah, L. (1988). The Noun Class System of Bafaw. A Maitrise Project, University of Yaounde.

Ferguson, Charles (1963). Assumptions about Nasals: A sample study in Phonological Universals. In John Greenberg (ed.), Universals of Language, 53-60. Cambridge University Press.

Ferguson, Charles (1975). "Universal Tendencies and 'Normal' nasality" In Larry Hyman and John Ohala (eds), Nasalfest: Papers from a symposium on Nasals and Nasalisation. 175-96. Sandford: Sandford University press, New York, (1979).

Goldsmith, J. (1976). *Autosegmental phonology*. Cambridge, Mass: MIT PhD Dissertation. Distributed by Indiana University Linguistics Club. Published by Garland Press, New York, (1979).

Hyman, L. M. (1975) *Phonology: Theory and Analysis*. London: Holt Rinehart and Winston.

Neba, Ayu'nwi (1998). *Tone in the Bafut Noun Phrase*. An unpublished M.A. Thesis. University of Buea.

Neba, Ayu'nwi (2008). Constraints Interaction in Bafut Tonology. A PhD Dissertation. University of Buea.

Njume, C. (2000). On Wh-Operators in Nfaw. A B. A. Long Essay. University of Buea.

Rich, Furne. (1963). Arabela Phonemes and High-Level Phonemes and High-Level Phonology. Elson (ed). Studies in Peruvian Indian Languages I. Summer Institute of Linguistics Publications in Linguistics and Related Fields 9. Norman: Summer Institute of Linguistics and University of Oklahoma (193-206).

Ruhlen, Merritt. (1978) Nasal Vowels. In Joseph, Greenberg, (ed), Universals of Human Language 2: Phonology, Standard: University Press 203-41).

Chapter Three
The Noun Class System of Bafaw

Lydia E. Ebah, Ayu'nwi N. Neba & Emmanuel N. Chia

3.0 Introduction
This chapter describes the noun class system of the language. The classification is based on the traditional system of labelling noun classes in Bantu languages (Guthrie 1948:11, Meeussen, 1967). The work done here has as basis work on the classification of Bafaw nouns by Ebah (1990[1]). The criteria employed are:

1. The occurrence of the nouns with a specific set of concording elements.
2. The noun prefixes
3. The pairing of a certain class with another class as singular and plural.
   This criterion can of course not be applied when the singular/plural dichotomy is irrelevant (that is for a mass, abstract nouns and single class genders, etc.).

Even though there is evidence that nouns may be put into semantic groups (Welmers 1973:166), we do not use this as a primary criterion of classification. This is because there is no single class which contains only nouns of a particular semantic group.

Based on these factors, we identify 13 noun classes for this language with classes 1 and 6 having sub classes: 1a and 6a respectively. The various classes are described below.

3.1 Noun Class Prefixes
This class which one? Readjust the heading. has the proto Bantu prefix *mu and has two sub classes: the traditional class 1 which has the following prefixes occurring as allomorphs N,

and m^w; and the class 1a nouns which have no prefix. The two classes are illustrated below.

3.1.1 Class1: Proto Bantu (PB)*mu
Examples of nouns in this class are:

(1) a. m-ɔ́?   'person'   b. m^w-àlân   'daughter'
    m-ààɲà   'sibling' m^w-ǎn   'child'

   c. mù-mân   'son'   d. ŋ̀-kə̀n   'guest'
    mù-kálá   'whiteman'   ǹ-sún   'friend'

An observation of the data in (1) reveals that the class 1 nominal can be realized in four different ways m, m^w, mu and N. As we will see below, there is every reason for us to consider these nouns as belonging to the same class. For example, they take the same concords and form their plurals by taking the same morphological prefix. The theoretical question that arises is, given these allomorphs, which one of them is the basic morpheme and how do we account for the surface realizations. In other words, which of these morphemes does a learner of Bafaw or a child internalize?

In generative phonology (Chomsky and Halle 1968) when there are alternants as we have above, one of them is basic and the rest are derived from that one. As to which one of them is chosen as basic depends on a number of considerations some of which include: pattern congruity, simplicity, naturalness, predictability and economy (see Hyman 1975, Carr 1990, and Burquest 1998). In our analysis, we will make use of predictability.

A look at 1b and 1c reveals that m^w clearly precedes vowels. **mu** precedes consonants. If one were to base the analysis only on these two allomorphs, then it will be easy to postulate either a vowel deletion or a vowel insertion rule to account for these; and if this were to be the option, then vowel deletion would be the ultimate solution given that deletion is less costly than insertion (the generative grammar factor of simplicity). The rule in 2 below will therefore be postulated to account for this derivation.

2. /u/ →[w]/_____ v

This rule states that the high back round tense vowel devocalizes before a vowel.

The claim that this rule makes is that we can never have two contiguous vowels across morpheme boundaries in this language. This solution therefore assumes that **mu** is the basic morphemes for the class marker. This assumption gets its strength from the proto Bantu prefix for this class of nouns which is *mo given that it is natural and simple to move from this *mo to [mu] and then to [m^w]. However, this solution raises a number of questions when one looks at the data in 1a and 1c. The worry is: why does this same mu not turn to mw in 1a given that it also precedes vowels as in 1b? Instead, we will need to postulate a vowel deletion rule to account for these data. While vowel deletion is a natural process in Bantu languages, the context of deletion in this case is not evident. What is clear is that mu must be the basic allomorph. This is because as we move from 1a to 1b, there is always a prosodic evidence of the loss of some segmental material-the root vowel while the root initial vowel has a phonemic low tone. In cases where a low tone surfaces, we assume that the root vowel was originally low toned and the deletion of the prefix vowel leads to stray erasure of the resulting floating tone because it is identical with the root tone. Given this conclusion, the problem is how to derive the data in 1a.

Atindogbe (2006) grapples with this problem by appealing to the syllable structure of the root word. He argues that some of these alternations can be attributed to the fact that some of the roots have CVC structures. As we can see from the data in 1, it is evident that this is not true because anyone of the prefixes can be used in CVC structures.

An alternative solution that we propose here is motivated by McCarthy's (1991) templatic skeletal model which he uses to analyze Semitic languages. In this solution, we will attribute the alternation in the nominal prefix in 1a, 1b and 1c to the structure of the root. As we have already mentioned, the form in 1c is basic. The major problem is to answer the question why there is devocalization in 1b but deletion in 1a. the answer is that the nouns in 1b each have an empty C-slot in the root while those in 1a do not. When the prefix is attached to these two roots, the prefix vowel desyllabifies and dissociates from the prefix vowel. While this resulting floating vowel finds an empty C-slot to dock onto in 1b, it does not in 1a; the result is that it is deleted. The derivation in 3 below illustrates this.

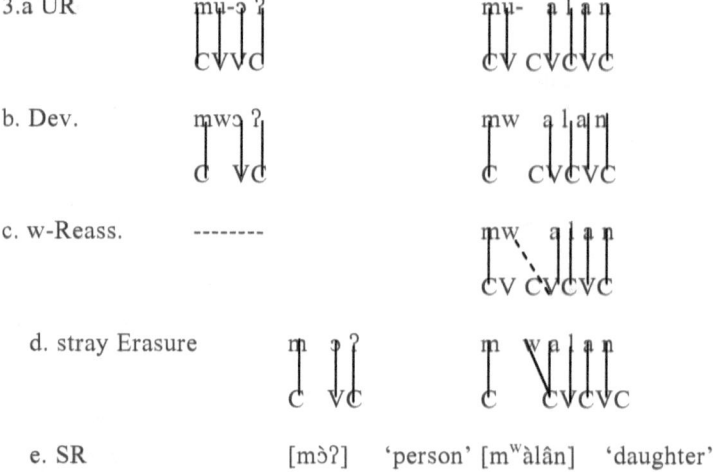

e. SR   [mɔ̂ʔ]   'person' [mʷàlân] 'daughter'

In 3a, we have the underlying representations of the words in 1a and 1b. As shown here, the roots in 3a have different initial structures. While the root of 'person' is VC, that of daughter is CVCVC. In other words, the root of 'person' does not have a floating C-slot. In 3b, the process of devocalization applies. This devocalization results in the delinking of the segment from its original C-slot. In 3c, the resulting floating glide reassociates to available C-slots. Since the root of 'daughter' has an empty C-slot, it lodges the floating glide while the root for 'person' cannot lodge its own glide because it lacks a floating C-slot. The result of this is that stray erasure erases it as it takes away every unassociated element in 3d. 3e is the surface representation.

With this problem solved, the next set of data is that in 1d where the prefix vowel is completely lost and the prefix surfaces with different place features as one moves from one word to another.

What we can say here is that this class of nouns has completely lost the vowel of the prefix, retaining only the nasal. This nasal then homogenizes with the root initial consonants in place of articulation. This phenomenon is common in Bantu linguistics.

To conclude, we have assumed that the basic morpheme for the class 1 prefix is mu and that the other surface alternants can be derived through the phonological processes of glide formation, historical vowel deletion and homorganic nasal assimilation.

Class 1a PB *Ø

Class 1a has a zero (Ø) prefix. According to Ebah (1990), most proper names, like it is the case with other Bantu languages occur in this class. Examples of nouns in this class are presented in 4.

4. Ø-sísɔ́   'father'
   Ø-àŋwá   'cat'
   Ø-àkʷɔ́   'Akwo'
   Ø-dìbó   'Dibo'
   Ø-èlɔ́ŋgè   'Elonge'

All these nouns take their plurals in class 2.

Class 2 PB *ba

The nouns that belong to this class have two phonetic forms as the data in 5 illustrate.

5 a. **bà-kálá**   'white people'   b. **b-á?**   'persons'
      bà-kə̀n   'guests'   **b-ààwà**   'siblings'
      bà-kʷí?   'widows'   **b- ăǹ**   'children'
      bà-sún   'friends'   **b-álân**   'daughters'
      bà-fɔ̀n   'chiefs'

As observed in the data, the class 2 nominal prefix can either be realized as [**bà**] (5a), or as [**b**], 5b. As it will be realized, all the noun roots in 5a where [**bà**] occurs have initial consonants while those in 5b where [**b**] occurs begin in vowels. It will be recalled that in chapter three (see 1.2.4.4?), we postulated a rule of vowel deletion in which the first of two contiguous vowels across morpheme boundaries gets deleted in fast speech. This is the same vowel deletion rule that applies in 5b to delete the vowel of the prefix. This means that the basic nominal prefix for class 2 is [**bà**].

It is important to mention at this point that we found that there are some class 1 nouns that take double plurals. This is illustrated in 6 below.

6 a. **mù-mân**   'son'   b. **bà-bù-mân** 'sons'

In 6a, we have a class 1 noun in isolation while 6b contains the plural of the noun. There is evidence that the class 1 nominal prefix is retained in the plural. What is interesting here is that the consonant of the nominal prefix changes from nasal to oral. Explanatorily, it looks like all the consonants in a compound prefix (single prefix made up of two independent prefixes) in this language must agree in nasality and it is the nasal quality of the leftmost consonant that spreads. Following suprasegmental phonology (Hyman 1975) and Autosegmental phonology (Goldsmith 1976) and its extensions (Goldsmith 1990, Kenstowicz 1994), this phenomenon can be analysed as shown in 7.

7a. UR   [-nas][+nas]
                    | |
                 [bà   mù]-mân

b. [-nas] spread   [-nas] [+nas]
    and [+nas] delink   ⌐--   =
                         bà   bù-mân

c. SR   [bàbùmân]   'son'

In 7a, the underlying representations of the prefixes are provided with the prefix boundaries indicated with brackets. In 7b, the feature [-nas] spreads from the outermost layer of the prefix unto the innermost shell, delinking any nasal feature originally associated to it. The resulting surface representation is shown in 7c with the consonant of the innermost shell of the prefix noun carrying an oral feature like the outermost layer.

Class 3: Proto Bantu *mu*

The behaviour of the class 3 nominal prefix is similar to that of class 1. It is ipso facto expected to exhibit three allomorphs: [N], [m] and [m^w]. These different prefixes are illustrated in 8 below.

8a. m-ìnyì   'bee'   b. ǹ-lá?   'branch'
    m^w-ìnyì   'tobacco'   ŋ̀-káŋgáá   'root'
                                   m̀-bɜ̀ŋmúké   'elbow'

The nouns in 8a illustrate the occurrence of [m] and [m^w]. It is important to note that these two nouns are single gender nouns. The nouns in 8b show that this prefix like the class 1 prefix also undergoes homorganic nasal assimilation.

Class 4: Proto Bantu *me*
The class 4 nominal prefix is [**mi-**]. Examples of nouns in this class are presented in 9 below. Class 3 nouns take their plurals in this class.

9. mì-lâʔ 'branches'
    mì-tôŋ 'colocacias'
    mì- káŋgáá 'roots'

Class 5: Proto Bantu *ne*
This prefix can be realised with two structures: either CV or C. The CV structure occurs before consonants while the C occurs before vowels. As we did for classes 1 and 3, the CV is basic while the C structure is derived through Vowel deletion. Phonetically, there are two ways of realising the prefix. It can either be [**lì**] or [**dì**]. Examples of these are presented in 10.

10a. lì-bɔ̀ʔ 'pumpkin'   b. dì-fé   'twin'
     lì-túmbá 'family'   d-ín   'name'
     lì-bîn   'testicle'   dì-sʷèʔdíké 'wrist'
                              dì-búʔ   'scorpion'

The nouns in 10a have the prefix [**lì-**] while those in 10b have the prefix [**dì-**]. From the data, it is not clear when we use any one of the prefixes. We consequently register them as two sub classes of class 5.

Class 6: Proto Bantu *ma*
The class 6 nominal prefix corresponds directly with the proto Bantu prefix ***ma**. Like in many other Bantu languages, most plural and mass nouns as well as liquids are attested in this class. Examples of nouns in this class are presented in 11.

11a. mà-bè   'livers'   b. mà-kíì   'blood'
     mà- bí 'faeces'   mà-nyâ   'siblings'
     mà-súŋ 'teeth'   mà-díʔ   'water'
     mà-túmbá 'families'   mà-dé   'river'
     mà-fín 'forest'   mà-ʃé   'stagnant water'

Nouns in this class are either mass nouns (nouns with no singulars like those in 11b) or plurals of class 5, 11, 13 and some class 7 nouns. It is worth noting that in Proto Bantu noun classification, the nouns in 11b are classified as class 6a. In Bafaw, there is no morphological motivation to break this class into classes 6 and 6a given that the two sets of nouns take the same phonetic nominal prefix, and exhibit the same concords. The only difference which is semantically motivated is the fact that the nouns in 11a have singulars while those in 11b do not.

Class 7: Proto Bantu *ke*
The class 7 nominal prefix is either realised as [e] or as [ɛ]. As we demonstrate below, it is not clear when to use the two alternants. This requires more investigation. It should however be pointed out that [ɛ] is more recurrent than [e]. Some nouns in this class take their plurals in class 6 while others take their plurals in class 8. Examples of these nouns are presented in 12 below.

12 a. è-búsà   'waist'   b. è-kfì   'thigh'
    è- kúlìkúlì 'butterfly'   è-bóŋbónsú   'lips'
    è -ʃɔ́ʔ   'feather'   è-fì   'bone'

Class 8: Proto Bantu *bi*
Most nouns in class 7 take their plurals in this class. The nominal prefix for this class is [bì]. Examples are presented in 13.

13. bì-kíʔ   'irons'
    bì-ʃǔm   'grass'
    bì- pún   'abscesses'
    bì- fáŋ   'animal tails'

Class 9: Proto Bantu *N*
Nouns in this class have a zero prefix. Most of the nouns in this class are animals, and insects. The class also contains nouns that are body parts. Examples are presented in 14.

14.   kʷí   'bush rat'

mbʷá	'dog'
kɔ́m	'monkey'
kûm	'snail'
pɔ́ɔ̀m	'chalk'

In some neighbouring languages like Denya (Mbuagbaw 2002) the nominal prefix is a homorganic nasal. In Nfaw as we have seen in 14, there are nouns that are clearly prefixless. However, there are many nouns in this class with root initial nasals. Given that this nasal is retained when these nouns take their plurals in class 10, we deemed it necessary to adopt the Ø-prefix hypothesis. The data in 14b and 14c show class 9 nouns and their corresponding plurals.

14b.	mbʷá	'dog'	c.	mbʷá	'dogs'
	ŋgwì	'pig'		ŋgwì	'pigs'
	ntɔ́	'wooden drum'		mà-dí?	'wooden drums'

Class 10: Proto Bantu *N
As mentioned above, nouns in class 9 take their plurals in class 10. The difference between these two classes of nouns can only be spotted in their concords. This will be demonstrated in the appropriate section. As examples, see the nouns in 14.

Class 11: Proto Bantu *lo
The nominal prefix for this class is [dù]. Only a limited number of nouns are attested in this class. When this prefix appears before a noun with an initial root vowel, it is either deleted by Vowel deletion or devocalised. Examples of nouns in this class are given in 15.

15.	dw-î	'nose'
	dw-ĭ	'latrine'
	dù-lú	'sun'
	dwɛ̀	'laughter'

These nouns take their plurals in class 6 whose prefix is [mà].

Class 13: Proto Bantu *vo

The nouns in this class are essentially miscellaneous, that is, they cannot in any way be associated with any semantic group. The nominal prefix here is phonetically realised as [wù], [wò] or [b^w]. As we will demonstrate, these phonetic realisations are allomorphs which can be analysed as deriving from the basic morpheme [wù] through the application of phonological rules. Before we discuss this in any detail, it is necessary to illustrate the occurrence of these allomorphs.

16.a. **wù-dúù** 'night'   b. **b^w- ǎlù** 'canoe'   c. **wò-wə̀** 'mountain'
   wù-kù 'mountain'   **b^w-ɔ́** 'medicine'
   wù-tì 'bed'   **b^w- ín** 'day'
   wù-kà? 'frince'   **b^w-ə̀** 'tree'

As observed in 16, [wù] occurs before noun roots with initial consonants while [b^w] precedes roots with initial vowels. Before we comment on the third alternant [wò] let us deal with the first two. We start off with the assumption that [wù] is the basic morpheme and that [b^w] is its derivative. Like we observed earlier, when a round vowel precedes another vowel, it devocalises to [w]. However, the resulting word initial [ww] is not allowed in the language. Consequently, the first [w] changes to [b] in order to maintain distinctiveness and licensing[2] constraints. The derivation is set out in 17.

17.   a. UR   **wù-álú**

      b. GF   **wwalu**

      c. b-Formation   **bwalu**

      d. Coalescence   **b^{w}alu**

      e. SR   [b^{w}ǎlù]   'canoe'

In 17a the underlying representations are provided. In 17b, glide formation takes place changing the round [**u**] vowel before an adjacent vowel to [**w**]. The [**ww**] sequence is avoided by the conversion of the first [**w**] to [**b**] in 17c. This process is followed by that of coalescence in which a [**bw**] sequence becomes [**b^w**]. Of course, the surface representation is provided in 17e. Two issues are in place here: first, the formulation of the b-formation rule and second, the ordering of rules.

The b-formation rule can be stated as shown in 18.

18. $\quad\quad\quad$ /w/ → [b]/_____w

In prose the rule states that the first of two voice labial velar approximants becomes plosives.

As far as rule ordering is concerned, it is obvious that glide formation must occur before b-formation so that it can create environments for the application of b-formation. The rules therefore are crucially ordered in a feeding relationship.

With regard to the data in 17c, we can explain that the prefix vowel [**u**] harmonises with the root [ə]. That is, it is lowered from a high vowel position to a mid position (that is from a high to a mid vowel) because of the root schwa. This is only a hypothesis as we did not find enough data to justify this assertion.

We must mention here that unlike in Ebah (1990) where this class is labelled 14, we have deemed it necessary to label it class 13. This is for the simple reason that in standard Bantu noun classification, odd numbers are assigned to singular classes while even numbers are assigned to plural classes. The nouns in this class are all singular and as we will see in the section under gender, they take their plurals in class 6. Given that there is no class 13 in this language, we prefer to assign these nouns to class 13.

Class 19: Proto Bantu *pi*

Class 19 like class 11 has very few nouns. Phonetically, the prefix is either realised as [fi-] or [fʲ-]. It is realised as [fi-] before consonants and as [fʲ-] before vowels. Most of the nouns that we found had only vowel initial roots but given an independent evidence that this language constantly avoids vowel clusters, it is logical to conclude that the [fʲ-] is a derivative of /fi-/.

19.   fʲ -ăŋgú?   'sand'
       fʲ –ĕŋ   'mushroom'
       fʲ –ɔ́?   'wild pepper'

It should be pointed out that most diminutive nouns are found in this class and most of them take their plurals in class 6. In brief, these are all the noun prefixes that we were able to find for this language. In the following sections we are going to synoptically comment on the concord and gender systems of the language.

3.2 The Noun Class Genders

The nouns described above frequently pair up as singular and plural. This pairing is commonly known as genders. Abstract and mass nouns such as strength, blood and water, for which enumeration is irrelevant are considered as single class gender or neuter. On the other hand, nouns like child, head, butterfly, etc, which have a singular/plural distinction are termed double class genders. The double genders of Nfaw can be summarily presented as follows: 1(a)/2, ¾, 5/6, 7/8 7/6, 9/10, 11/6, 13/6. The graphic figure in 20 illustrates this.

20.

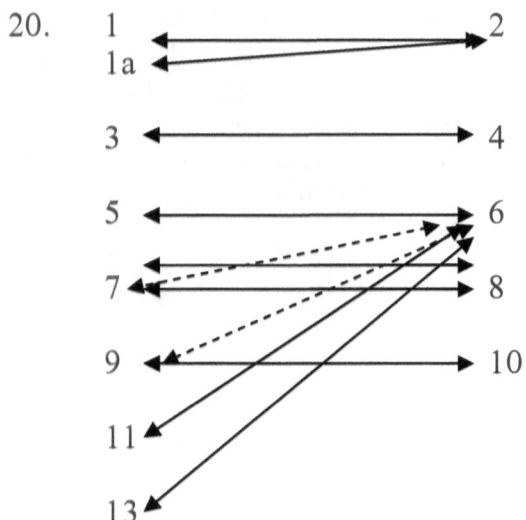

From this table, it can be seen that class 6 is the most widely used plural. Four out of the eight singular classes namely 5, 7, 11 and 13 take their plurals in this class. The dotted lines indicate pairs with very few examples. In all, 9 double class genders are discernable in this language. The double class genders are presented in 21 below.

21. Gender 1(a)/2 **N-, Ø-, bà-**

mʷ-àlân	'daughter'	b-álân	'daughters'
mʷ-ăn	'child'	b-ăn	'children'
ǹ-sún	'friend'	bà-sún	'friends'
m-ɔ̀ʔ	'person'	b-áʔ	'persons'
m-àànyà	'sibling'	b-àànyà	'siblings'
ǹ-tâŋ	'slave'	bà-tân	'slaves'
ǹ-dʒúm	'husband'	a-ǹ-dʒúm	'husbands'
ŋ̀-kɔ̀n	'guest'	bà-kɔ̀n	'guests'
Ø-sísɔ́	'father'	bà-sísɔ́	'fathers'
Ø-àŋwá	'cat'	b-àŋwá	'cat'
Ø-sápwɔ̂	'mouse'	ba-sápwɔ̂	'mice'

Gender 3/4 N-, mì-

ŋ̀-kí	'village'	mì-kí	'villages'
m̀-bʲà?	'language'	mì-bʲà?	'languages'
m̀-fɔ́n	'handle'	mì-fɔ́n	'handles'
ǹ-Ɛ̀ŋgà	'thread'	mì-Ɛ̀ŋgà	'threads'
ǹ-ðZì	'boundary'	mì-ðZì	'boundaries'
ǹ-túm	'walking stick'	mì-túm	'walking sticks'
ǹ-sàm	'event'	mì-sàm	'events'
ǹ-dìm	'grave'	mì-dìm	'graves'
m̀-bá?	'parcel'	mì-bá?	'parcels'

Gender 5/6 lì-/dì-, mà-

lì-bùm	'abdomen'	mà-bùm	'abdomens'
lì-lámbá	'buttock'	mà-lámbá	'buttocks'
lì-súŋ	'tooth'	mà-súŋ	'teeth'
lì-jà	'birth'	mà-jà	'births'
lì-sèsú	'comb'	mà-sèsú	'combs'
lì- wá	'death'	mà- wá	'deaths'
lì-túmbá	'family'	mà-túmbá	'families'
dì-fé	'twin'	mà-fé	'twins'

Gender 7/8 e/è-/, bì-

è-pəŋ	'thigh'	bì- pə́ŋ	'thghs'
è-jem̀	'tongue'	bì-jém	'tongues'
è-tú	'shoulder'	bì-tú	'shoulders'
è-sɔ́?	'porcupine prong'	bì- sɔ́?	'porcupine prong s'
è-támb í	'shoe'	bì-támbí	'shoes'
è-jàlà	'word'	bì-jàlà	'words'
è-wú	'death ceremony'	bì-wú	'death ceremonies'

Gender 7/6 e/è-/, mà-
Only two examples were found for this gender in our research.

è-ké	'hand'	mà-ké	'hands'
è-kʷì	'leg'	mà-kʷì	'legs'

Gender 9/10 ø-, ø-

kʷí	'bush rat'	kʷí	'bush rats'
mbʷá	'dog'	mbʷá	'dogs'
kə́m	'monkey'	kə́m	'monkeys'
kûm	'snail'	kûm	'snails'
pɔ́ə̀m	'chalk'	pɔ́ə̀m	'pieces of chalk'

Gender 9/8 ø-, bì-

jó?	'boil'	bì-jó?	'boils'
kúkwèlí?	'tortoise'	bì- kúkwèlí?	'tortoises'

Gender 11/6 dù-, mà-

This gender is interesting in that like gender 9/10, the singular prefix is not replaced in the plural.

dʷî	'nose'	mà-dʷî	'noses'
dʷɪ̂	'latrine'	mà-dʷɪ̂	'latrines'

Looking at these words, one would want to say that the prefix is not marked (ø-). This is not possible given that generative grammar excludes predictable material in the underlying representation. We therefore have no other option but to postulate [dù-] as the singular nominal prefix. More evidence is got from the single gender nouns like [**dùlù**] 'sun' which has an overt [du-]. The numeral concord for all these nouns as shown in section 3 below is [dí-].

Gender 13/6 wù-/bʷ-, mà-

wù-dúù	'night'	mà-dúù	'nights'
wù-kù	'mountain'	mà-kù	'mountains'
wù-tì	'bed'	mà-tì	'beds'
wù-ká?	'fence'	mà-ká?	'fences'
wù-jà?	'pangolin'	mà-jà?	'pangolins'
wò-wɔ́	'marriage'	mà-wɔ́	'marriages'
bʷ-ɔ̀	'tree'	mà-bʷɔ̀	'trees'

It should be noted that whereas the plural mà- replaces the wù- singular prefix in most of the items above, this is not true of the last item. The mà- prefix is instead a sort of double prefix to the singular prefix bʷ-.

As far as single class genders are concerned, the following classes have nouns which either have only a singular or a plural. These classes are 1a, 3, 5, 6, 6a, 7, 11, 13, and 19. These single class genders are presented below.

Gender 1a ø-
Most of the nouns in this gender are proper names.

Ø-ŋgɔ̀	'Ngoh'
Ø-sónà	'Sona'
Ø-èpʲɛ̀	'Epie'
Ø-dìbó	'Dibo'
Ø-èlàŋgwè	'Elangwe'
Ø-àkámà	'Akama'

Gender 3 N-
m̀-búmbú	'ash'
ǹ-dùkú	'bush'
ǹ-júmbí	'oil trough'

Gender 5 lì-
lì-fĩʔ	'pus'
lì-bàn	'poverty'
lì-bàŋ	'fog'
lì-sín	'moon'
lì-fɔ́ŋ	'fat'
lì-bì	'breast milk'

Gender 6 mà-
These nouns are plural nouns without singulars. They include the following nouns:

mà-káŋgá	'chest'
mà-fíndù	'soot'
mà-kún	'beans'
mà-túm	'lies'
mà-sàkán	'thanks'
mà-díʔ	'water'
mà-kĩ̀	'blood'
mà-dé	'river'

Gender 7 è-
- è- túmán   'fufu'
- è-sàkâ   'melon'
- è-lén   'palm leaves'
- è-dúbé   'honour'
- è-dìlím   'shadow'
- è-dí?   'sweat'
- è-kúl   'storm'

Gender 11 dù-
- dù-lú   'sun'
- dʷ-è   'laughter'

Gender 11 dù-
- wù-júì   'honey'
- wù-kʷǎ   'salt'
- wù-ndì   'rice'
- wù-jɔ́   'sleep'
- wù-dì?   'weight'
- wù-sɔ̀ŋ   'shame'
- wù-jà?   'length'

Gender 19 fì-
- fʲ-ǎŋgú?   'sand'
- fʲ-ěŋ   'mushroom'
- fʲ-ɔ̀?   'wild pepper'
- fì-ì   'cam wood'

3.3 Concord Markers

In section 2, we put some nouns which have the same phonetic forms in different classes. Examples of such classes are 9 and 10. The guide to this grouping was the use of concordial markers. Two nouns may have the same phonetic material but take different concords and ipso facto be classified as belonging to different classes. This section of the paper examines concords. The tables which follow summarise the concords of the different noun classes presented in section 2. We have presented the following concords here: the numeral concord, the possessive pronoun concords, demonstratives and associative concords.

22. Numeral Concords for the 13 Nfaw Noun Classes

Class	Example	one -fɔ́/-pɔ́	two -bè	three -làán	four -níìn	five -t âŋ	how many -tèíŋ
1.	ǹdʒíb 'thief'	ǹfɔ́					
2.	bàsún 'friends'		bàbè	bàlàán	bàníìn	bà tâŋ	bàtèíŋ
3.	m̀màŋ 'kernel'	ǹfɔ́					
4.	mìkɔ̀? 'ropes'		mìbè	mìlàán	mìníìn	mì tâŋ	mìtèíŋ
5.	lìkə̀? 'egg'	lìfɔ́					
6.	màbɔ̀? 'pumkins'		màbè	màlàán	mànííìn	màtâŋ	màtèíŋ
7.	èfì 'bone'	èfɔ́					
8.	bìkàkán 'insects'		bìbè	bìlàán	bìníìn	bìtâŋ	bìtèíŋ
9.	m̀búl 'goat'	pɔ́					
10.	kʷí 'bush rats'		èbè	èlàán	èníìn	ètâŋ	ètèíŋ
11.	dʷí 'latrine'	dìfɔ́					
13.	bʷí n 'bush rats'	ùfɔ́					
19.	fɔ́?à 'thief'	pɔ́					

An examination of the concords in table 22 reveals that in the main, the concord marker is identical with nominal prefix of the noun. Notice that the concord for 'one' in classes 9 and 19 changes from [fɔ́] in the other 11 classes, to [pɔ́] in these two classes. An interesting thing to notice is with class 10 nouns. Recall that we said earlier that class 10 nouns are prefixless, but also observed that there was evidence that many nouns in this class have initial nasals, suggesting that the nasal prefix noticed in other Bantu languages might just be phasing out in this language. When one examines the concords above, one notices that the class 10 numeral concord is [è] for 'two', 'four', and 'how many'; similar to the concord of class 7 which has [è] as nominal prefix. As a general observation, the numeral concord is identical with the nominal prefix both segmental and prosodically. However, this takes exception in classes 9, 13, and 19. When the noun does not have a phonetic prefix, the numeral concord is [è]. Table 23 shows the possessive concord.

23. Possessive Concords for the 13 Nfaw Noun Classes

Class	Example	my	Your	his/her	our	your	their
1.	mʷăn 'child'	mʲə̂	wɔ̂	mɔ̂	sè	nʲê	bɔ̂
2.	băn 'children'	bámʲə̂	bá wɔ̂	bá mɔ̂	básè	bá nʲê	bábɔ̂
3.	ǹlâ? 'branch'	ḿmʲə̂	ḿ wɔ̂	ḿ mɔ̂	ńsè	ńnʲê	ḿbɔ̂
4.	mìlâ? 'branches'	mímʲə̂	mí wɔ̂	mí mɔ̂	mísè	mínʲê	míbɔ̂
5.	lìpà? 'wing'	límʲə̂	lí wɔ̂	lí mɔ̂	lísè	línʲê	líbɔ̂
6.	màpà? 'wings'	mámʲə̂	máwɔ̂	mámɔ̂	má	mánʲê	mábɔ̂
7.	èjɔ̀ŋ 'age group'	émʲə̂	é wɔ̂	émɔ̂	ésè	énʲê	ébɔ̂
8.	Bìjɔ̀ŋ 'age groups'	bímʲə̂	Bíwɔ̂	bímɔ̂	bísè	bínʲê	bíbɔ̂
9.	kʷí 'bush rat'	èmʲə̂	è wɔ̂	èmɔ̂	èsè	ènʲê	èbɔ̂
10.	kʷí 'bush rats'	émʲə̂	é wɔ̂	émɔ̂	ésè	énʲê	ébɔ̂
11.	dʷí 'latrine'	dímʲə̂	dí wɔ̂	dímɔ̂	dísè	dínʲê	díbɔ̂
13.	wùdʷí 'latrines'	úmʲə̂	ú wɔ̂	úmɔ̂	úsè	únʲê	úbɔ̂
19.	fàŋgú 'sand'	úmʲə̂	ú wɔ̂	úmɔ̂	úsè	únʲê	úbɔ̂

The possessive concord for class 1 is not marked. In other words, there is no possessive concord for class 1 nouns as shown in table 23. Apart from this, the pattern is almost the same as the one in table 22. What is however clear here is that [è-] surfaces here as the concord for classes 9, and 10. The only difference is that while it is low toned in class 9, it is high toned in class 10. Classes 13 and 19, on their part, have [ú-] as possessive concord.

24. Qualifier Concords for the Nfaw Noun Classes

class	good	all of it	the big one	the small one	which one	another
1.	èmbáá	ánsʲ ə̂n	Ánnə́n	ántékə́ŋ	ánfɔ́	ámpɔ́ɔ́?
2.	bámbáá	básʲ ə̂n	Bánə́n	bátékə́ŋ	báfɔ́	bá pɔ́ɔ́?
3.	múmbáá	músʲ ə̂n	Múnə́n	mútékə́ŋ	múfɔ́	múpɔ́ɔ́?
4.	mímbáá	mísʲ ə̂n	Mínə́n	mítékə́ŋ	mífɔ́	mí pɔ́ɔ́?
5.	límbáá	lísʲ ə̂n	Línə́n	lítékə́ŋ	lífɔ́	lí pɔ́ɔ́?
6.	mámbáá	másʲ ə̂n	Mánə́n	mátékə́ŋ	máfɔ́	mápɔ́ɔ́?
7.	símbáá	sísʲ ə̂n	Sínə́n	sítékə́ŋ	sífɔ́	sípɔ́ɔ́?
8.	bémbáá	bésʲ ə̂n	Bénə́n	bétékə́ŋ	béfɔ́	bépɔ́ɔ́?
9.	èmbáá	èsʲ ə̂n	Ɛnə́n	ètékə́ŋ	èfɔ́	èpɔ́ɔ́?
10.	émbáá	ésʲ ə̂n	Ɛ́nə́n	étékə́ŋ	éfɔ́	épɔ́ɔ́?
11.	dímbáá	dísʲ ə̂n	Dínə́n	dítékə́ŋ	dífɔ́	dípɔ́ɔ́?
13.	wúmbáá	wúsʲ ə̂n	Wúnə́n	wútékə́ŋ	wúfɔ́	wúpɔ́ɔ́?
19.	úmbáá	úsʲ ə̂n	Únə́n	útékə́ŋ	úfɔ́	úpɔ́ɔ́?

The table in 24 shows concord markers when nouns from different classes are collocated with different kinds of adjectives. The revelation here is that the concords are identical with the nominal prefixes. Unlike the other concords that we have seen so far, there is no variation between the prefixes and the qualifier concords.

25. Demonstrative Concords for the 13 Nfaw Noun Classes

class	example	gloss	that/those mentioned	This one	That one
1.	ǹdʒíb	'thief'	Áwɔ̂	àním	àníní
2.	bàsún	'friends'	ábʷɔ̂	bán	bání
3.	m̀bá?	'parcel'	έmmɔ̀	mún	múní
4.	mìkɔ̀?	'ropes'	έmmʲɔ̀	mín	míní
5.	lìkɔ̀?	'egg'	édʲɔ̀	dín	díní
6.	màbɔ̀?	'pumkins'	έmmɔ̀	mán	mání
7.	èfì	'bone'	Ɛjɔ̀	jín	jíní
8.	bìkàkán	'insects'	Bíbɔ̀	bín	bíní
9.	m̀búl	'goat'	Ɛjɔ̀	éním	èníní
10.	kʷí	'bush rats'	Ɛjɔ̀	jén	jéní
11.	dʷí	'latrine'	ǝdɔ̀	dín	díní
13.	wùkù	'mountain'	ɔ́bʷɔ̂	bún	búní
19.	fʲɔ̀?	'mushroom'	ɔ́bʷɔ̂	bún	búní

The table in 25 illustrates a number of demonstratives collocated with nouns from the various noun classes. As shown on the table, interesting things seem to be happening with the first column which contains definite demonstratives. The first general observation is that all but the class 8 concords have initial vowels which nevertheless vary as one moves from one class to the other. It is [à] for classes 1 and 2, [è] for classes 2, 6, 5, 7, 9 and 10; and [ə] for classes 11, 13, and 19. What we realise is that once the concordal vowel is prefixed to the CV nominal prefixes, the vowel of the nominal prefix drops to obtain the definite concord. This probably explains why the consonant of the nominal prefix is always present in the concord of the definite demonstrative. As for the concords of 'this' and 'that', it would be noticed that the pattern is fairly similar with those already discussed. That is, the concord bears the nominal prefix. The new discoveries though, are that classes 7 and 10 concords surface with initial glides [j] which was not noticed in the other concords. Classes 13 and 19 which up till now have surfaced with initial vowels in the other concords have surfaced here with an initial consonant, even though the vowel noticed in the other concords is retained after the bilabial plosive.

3.4 The Genitive Concord

The genitive construction is one which can literally be translated as 'N1 of N2'. The first noun (N1) is possessed by the second noun (N2). The genitive marker has its insitu position between the two nouns. This marker varies according to the noun class of the head noun. The examples in 26 below illustrate the different genitive markers. As the examples demonstrate, the associative markers (AM) share some phonetic similarities with the prefix of the first noun. They behave in the same way as the other concords already discussed. The new feature that can be noticed is that class 19 surfaces with and [έ] as the concord marker when it has always surfaced with [ú] before now.

26. i. m^w ăn   mú ǹ   fɔ̀n   'the chief's child'
        Cl_1 child AM Cl_1 chief

    ii. bà kə̀n   bá ǹ   fɔ̀n   'the chief's guest'
        Cl_2 guest AM Cl_1 chief

    iii. ǹ lú   mú ǹ   fɔ̀n   'the roof of the chief's house'
         Cl_3 roof AM Cl_1 chief

    iv. mì kàŋgáá mí b^w ə̀   'roots of a tree'
        Cl_4 child AM Cl_2 tree

    v. lì bî   lí ɲ̀   ɲà?   'the breast of a cow'
        Cl_5 breast AM Cl_9 cow

    vi. mà bî   má ḿ   búl   'the droppings of a goat'
        Cl_6 faeces AM Cl_9 goat

vii. è nìŋgán ɛ́ mà fɛ̂   'the twin's affinity'
    Cl_7 love AM Cl_6 twin

viii. bì lɔ̂ʔ bí bà fɔ̂n   'the title holders' spears'
     Cl_8 spear AM Cl_2 chief

ix. ŋ̀ gínʲà è dì lɛ́   'hardness of stone'
    Cl_9 strength AM Cl_5 stone

x. m̀ bʷá ɛ́ ǹ sòŋgòsòŋgò   'a hunter's dog'
   Cl_{10} dog AM Cl_9 hunter

xi. dʷ è dí mù nʲèŋè   'laughter of joy'
    Cl_{11} laughter AM Cl_3 joy

xii. wù lám ú sʷɔ́   'the first trap'
     Cl_{13} trap AM Cl_9 first

xiii. fʲ ə̀ŋ ɛ́ fɔ̂n   'mushroom of yesterday'
      Cl_{13} mushroom AM yesterday (Cl_{19})

27. Summary of Concords

class	numeral	possessive	demonstrative	Qualifier	Relative Pron.	Genitive
1.	ǹ-	ø-	áw-, ání-	ɛ́-, á-, áń-	á-	mú-
2.	bà-	bá-	áb-, bá-	bá-	á-	bá-
3.	ǹ-	ḿ-	ɛ́m-, mú-	mú-	ɛ́-	mú-
4.	mì-	mí-	ɛ́mí-, mí-	mí-	ɛ́m-	mí-
5.	lì-	lí-	ɛ́dʲ-, dí-	lí-	ɔ́-	lí-
6.	mà-	má-	ɛ́m-, má-	má-	ɛ́m-	má-
7.	è-	ɛ́-	ɛ́j-, jí-	sí-, sʲɛ́-	ɛ́-	ɛ́-
8.	bì-	bí-	bíb-, bí-	bɛ́-	ɛ́-	bí-
9.	ø	è-	ɛ́j-, ɛ́ní-	ɛ́-	ɛ́-	è-
10.	è-	ɛ́-	ɛ́j-, jɛ́-	ɛ́-	ɛ́-	ɛ́-
11.	dì-	dí-	ɔ́d-, dí-	dí-	á-	dí-
13.	ù-	ú-	ɔ́b-, bú-	wú-	á-	ú-
19.	ø	ú-	ɔ́b-, bú-	ú-	á-	ɛ́-

The table in 26 summarises all the concords that we have identified in this section of the chapter.

3.5 Conclusion

This chapter set out to sketch the noun classes of Nfaw. We have realised that this language has 13 noun classes. It has nine double gender classes and nine single gender classes. It has also been established that some of the phonetic alternations in some class prefixes can be accounted for both diachronically and synchronically. The fall out of the chapter is that to identify the prefixes of the different classes, one needs to appeal to the phonology of the language. A number of concords have also been discussed and presented in the work. These are the numeral, possessive, qualifier, demonstrative and genitive concords.

Notes

1. In fact, all the data presented here are drawn from that work. The classification is only slightly modified.

2. As argued in the literature (see Goldsmith 1990), the syllable onset position is a prosodic licenser and it cannot assign the same feature twice. We believe therefore that it is due to this reason that the first of the two consonants [ww] changes to [b].

References

Atindogbe, G. G. (2002). "Accounting for Prenasals in Bantu Languages of Zone A" Occasional Papers, No 14. Communications of the Centre for Advanced Studies of African Society. Cape Town: CASAS.

Burquest, D.A. (1998). *Phonological Analysis: A Functional Approach.* Texas: SIL: 31-80.

Carr Philip (1993). Phonological Analysis. Macmillan Press Lit. London

Chomsky, N. and Morris Halle (1968). The Sound Pattern of English. New York: Harper &Row.

Ebah, L. (1990). The Noun Class System of Bafaw. A Maitrise Project, University of Yaounde.

Goldsmith, J. (1976). *Autosegmental phonology*. Cambridge, Mass: MIT PhD Dissertation. Distributed by Indiana University Linguistics Club. Published by Garland Press, New York, (1979).

Guthrie, M. (1967-71). *Comparative Bantu* (4 vols.). Farnborough, Hants: Gregg.

Hyman, L. M. (1975) *Phonology: Theory and Analysis*. London: Holt Rinehart and Winston.

Kenstowicz, Michael. (1994). *Phonology in generative grammar*. Cambridge: Blackwell.

McCarthy, John. and Prince, A. (1991). The Phonetics and Phonology of Semitic Languages. Papers in Laboratory Phonology III. Phonological Structure and Phonetic Form, ed. By P. Keating. London: Cambridge University Press.

Meeussen, A. E. (1967). *Bantu grammatical reconstructions*. (Annales du Musée Royal de L'Afrique Centrale, Série 8, Sciences Humaines, 61.81-121). Tervuren: Musée Royal de l'Afrique.

Welmers, W. (1973) African Language Structures. Berkeley and Los Angeles. University of California *Press*.

Chapter Four
The Verb Morphology of Nfaw

Michael E. Apuge & Ayu'nwi N. Neba

4.0 Introduction
It has been demonstrated in the literature (see Meeussen 1967, Mutaka 1990, Mutaka and Tamanji 2000, Nurse (2003) etc. that the Bantu verb is complex containing the verb root and other morphemes- prefixes and suffixes While this complexity is conspicuous as one moves Eastwards (Narrow Bantu languages), many of the Bantu languages towards the West (Wide Bantu, especially Grassfields languages) have lost many of these morphemes leaving behind, in many cases, only vestiges in the form of floating tones (Leroy 1979, Asongwed and Hyman 1976, Hyman and Tadadjeu 1976) which attest to these once existing morphemes. Meeussen (1967) quoted in Nurse (2003:90) summarises the verbal word as shown in 1.

1. Initial-Subject-Negative-T (A)-Object# Root-Extension(s)-Final-Suffix

Nurse notes that all the slots to the left and right of root-Extensions in (1) involve verbal inflections. The initial expresses only two categories common to many Bantu languages, negative and relative but that individual languages express a range of other categories at Initial because this is a slot where new material often becomes grammaticalized. The Extension involves a closed and small set of valency-changing categories, of which causative, applicative, stative, reciprocal, reversive, and passive are the most common. The Final also includes a small, closed set originally having to do with mood and aspect but now including tense and aspect in some languages. The Suffix includes only a marker of imperative plural.

Schadeberg (2003:71) on his part observes that a typical verbal word form in Bantu consists of a stem preceded by one or more bound morphemes. The verbal stem may have prefixes specifying, amongst other things, the person or noun class of the subject as well as inflectional categories (such as time, aspect, negation etc.). The stem initial-position often has special stress-related phonological properties (tone, length, and vowel quality). A verbal stem, he notes, can be further divided into a verbal base (B) and a final suffix (F). This literature review makes the case that in talking about the verb and its morphology in any Bantu language, attention will need to be paid to tense, aspect, mood, negation, imperative markers and even the infinitive markers. It will also be necessary to look at valency-changing categories, such as causative, applicative, stative, reciprocal, reversive, and passive. In the discussion that follows we describe the Bafaw verb with these items in mind.

It is important to underscore that in coastal Bantu, the group of languages to which Nfaw belongs, such verbal satellites as those listed in 1 above have adopted various forms and do combine with the root in different ways for various semantic reasons. In this chapter, we examine the Nfaw verb, the distribution of its satellites and the effects that these satellites cause on the entire verb phrase. It is important to note that the treatment of the verb here adopts a functional approach. The chapter discusses mainly morphological issues that is, only the verb satellites which attach to the verb as either prefixes or suffixes. The next chapter focuses on those verbal elements which are purely syntactic.

The discussion is structured into eight sections. In §1 the verb root is examined vis a vis syllable structure. The imperative and the infinitive are presented in §2. In §3 verb classes are discussed. Since tense, aspect and mood constitute part of the verbal complex, we examine tense and aspect in § 4 and 5 respectively, while mood and modality are treated in § 6. In § 7 verbal extensions are discussed and the conclusion of the work is presented in §8.

4.1 The Verb Root and Syllable Structure
As mentioned in chapter two, the preferred syllable structure in Nfaw is CV with only sonorants capable of occupying the coda position. The Nfaw verb can either be mono-syllabic or disyllabic. We present the different verbs according to syllable structure below.

4.1.1 Monosyllabic verbs
There are two kinds of monosyllabic uninflected verb roots: CV as in 2a and CVC as in 2b.

2. a. lá "hit/beat"
   tú "tie"
   ʤĭ "cry"
   mwá "to drink"
   nya "to defecate"

   b. wún "plant"
   kúm "cook"
   yan "buy"
   wăn "fight"

The second set of verbs is disyllabic verbs which are shown in 3. A majority of the verbs in this language belong in this group of verbs. Those in 3a have the structure CV-CV while those in 3b have either CV-CVC, CVC-CV or CVC-CVC.

3. a. na-li "sleep"
   bú-lu "kill"
   gbé-li "break"
   fùmú "fly"

   b. búŋ-gú "run"
   sam-ban "greet"
   kún-dí "fall"
   shú-mán "sit"

4.1.2 Imperatives and Infinitives
In order to lay the groundwork for the discussion that follows, it is important to note essentials about the infinitive and the imperative form of the Nfaw verb so as to have an idea about the basic structure of the verb.

To begin with, the infinitive form of the verb in Nfaw comprises an infinitive marker **ádí** (with a H tone on both syllables) which precedes the verb root. Examples of these are given in 4. Hedinger (2004) observes that the initial [á] of the infinitive marker is a class 5 nominal prefix. Examples include:

4) a. ádí nali "to sleep"
    b. ádí wún "to plant"
    c. ádí yan "to buy"
    d. ádí mwá "to drink"
    e. ádí mɔ́n "to plait"
    f. ádí nya "to defecate"
    g. ádí wan "to fight"
    h. ádí kani "to think"
    i. ádí lá "to play/hit"
    j. ádí búlu "to kill"
    k. ádí gbéli "to break"

In this form of the verb, the verb roots have no inflections. This can be contrasted with the imperative forms of these verbs which have no independent segmental morphemes (for the imperative). The verb root in the infinitive can therefore be considered as the basic form of the Nfaw verb[1]

The imperative forms of the verbs in 2 are given in 3 below.

4) a. nalí "sleep"
    b. wún "plant"
    c. yăn "buy"
    d. mwă "drink"

    e. nyă "harvest"
    g. wăn "fight"
    h. lá "play/hit"

An observation of these data reveals that all the verbs end with an H tone even when their counterparts in 3 may end in L tone. This detail makes us conjecture that the imperative marker in this language must be a floating H tone which docks onto the final syllable of the root. For the verbs that end in H tones in 3, we will demonstrate below that they belong in the H tone verbs. Having justified our decision about the basic verb structure, we now turn to verb classification.

4.2 Verb Classes in Nfaw
Verbs in Nfaw can be put into a number of functional and structural classes. We consider these classes below.

4.2.1 Structural Classification (Verb Valency based Classification)
The classification here is based on the number of arguments that a verb can take. According to Bearth (2003), the structural and semantic sub classification of Bantu verbs is a principal key to understanding elementary syntactic structure. He notes that the first criterion from a primarily structural view to consider is the number of nominal phrases or arguments which are required or allowed to occur in combination with a given verb or class of verbs by virtue of the latter's inherent lexico-semantic properties- their valencies. As Bearth (2003:122) notes for Bantu, simple non-derived verbs in Nfaw can be put into three classes on the basis of the number of arguments that they can take. We consider these below.

4.2.1.1 One Place Predicates
These are verbs which express an action or state as limited to the agent or subject, or as ending in itself. In other words, such verbs do not necessitate an object to complete the intended meaning of an expression. Examples are given in (4).

(5) a. Ngoh   a   nalí
    Ngoh SM   sleep/ PT
    "Ngoh slept"

   b. Ngoh   a   fumú
      Ngoh SM   fly/ PT
      "Ngoh flew (away)"

Notice that the subject is always followed by a resumptive pronoun which we label here as a subject marker (SM). The SM is not counted as an argument because it is simply a repetition of the lexical subject.

4.2.1.2 Two Place Predicates

Two place verbs express an action as not limited to the agent or subject, but directed upon an object as well. That is, such verbs take a direct object or complement in addition to the subject. They can be called two argument verbs. Examples and their usage are shown in 5. 6) a. Ngoh

a. búlú   mbul
    Ngoh SM   kill/ PT   goat
    "Ngoh killed a goat"

b. Epie a   du   ɛ́ku
    Epie SM close/ PT door
    "Epie closed the door"

The acts of ''killing'' and ''closing'' are respectively construed as directed upon their corresponding direct objects.

4.2.1.3 Three Place Predicates

This class of verbs triggers the use of two objects for the construction in which the verb is used to be grammatical. In other words, such verbs express an action that involves the subject, direct object, and an indirect object. This class of verbs requires particular attention because it is not clear whether the last noun phrase can be treated as an argument or as part of a prepositional phrase. As we see in example 7a, there is an overt preposition separating the direct object while in 7b the two nouns are stringed together in object position. The decision is difficult to make because there are no object markers in Nfaw that will distinguish verb objects from prepositional objects as it is the case with other languages (see Tallerman 1998).

(7) a. Epie a   bek-í   káati á Ngoh
       Epie SM give PT book to Ngoh
       ''Epie gave the book to ngoh''

   b. Epie a   fatán-í   ban   póli
      Epie SM tell   PT children story
      ''Epie told children a story''

4.3 Tonal Classification

As mentioned in chapter two of this volume, Nfaw like other Bantu languages is a tone language. Verbs in these languages usually pattern into two tone classes (see Meeussen 1967, Mutaka 1990 etc.). Similarly, Nfaw verbs can also be classified into two tonal groups.

The two tonal verb classes are discussed below.

4.3.1 High Tone Roots

High tone verbs carry H tones on all their syllables. Examples are given in 8 below (all the verbs are given in the infinitive form since as mentioned above, verb roots are usually uninflected in this form).

(8) a. wún "plant"
    b. lá "hit/beat"
    c. kíndʒí "dry"
    d. tú "tie"
    e. kúm "cook"

These verbs maintain this High tone in the infinitive form as illustrated by the data in (9).

(9) a. ádí wún "to plant"
    b. ádí lá "to hit/beat"
    c. ádí kíndʒí "to dry"
    d. ádí tú "to tie"
    e. ádí kúm "to cook"

4.3.2 Low Tone Verbs

The low tone verbs surface with a LH melody in the imperative and unlike the H tone verbs, they surface with an L melody in the infinitive. Examples are listed in (9) imperatives and (10) for their corresponding infinitives.

(9) a. yǎn "buy"
    b. wǎn "fight"
    c. dʒǐ "cry"
    d. nǎn "chase"
    e. tǐ "write"

These verbs surface with LH melodies because as mentioned above, the imperative marker is a floating H tone which docks to the final vowel of the word. In the infinitive form (10), the imperative marker is no longer present and as a result, the verb roots surface with L tones.

(10) a. ádí wan "to fight"
 b. ádí dʒi "to cry"
 c. ádí fumu "to fly"
 d. ádí nali "to sleep"
 e. ádí fuma "to sit"

4.4 Tense in Nfaw

Tense is a grammatical category that specifies the time of an event or action. In other words, tense relates the time of the situation referred to, to some other time, usually to the moment of speaking (Comrie, 1976). The commonest tense found in languages- though not all languages distinguish these three tenses, or indeed distinguish tense at all – are past, present and future. Some languages, like Kom and many other Grassfields Bantu languages may have as many as eight distinct tenses (Chia 1976), Mfonyam (1989).

While it is evident that tense in this language is morphological, its analysis is not straightforward. This is because while it is clearly marked on some verbs, it is not evident in other verbs. However, while it is certain that Nfaw speakers can distinguish different times in which an event takes place, our analysis reveals that the language only makes a distinction between past and non-past tenses.

4.4.1 The Simple Past Tense

This tense is used to describe events and actions that occur prior to the time of speaking. Although not apparent on all the surface forms, the past tense in Nfaw seems to have a unique morpheme - /i/, which is a final vowel on the verb form as shown in (11a) below. What obtains in (11b-c) will be discussed after considering the data in table 1.

(11) a. Ngoh a kúnd-i
Ngoh sm sleep PT
"Ngoh slept"

b. Ngoh a búlú mbul
Ngoh Sm kill/ PT goat
"Ngoh killed a goat"

c. Ngoh a fumú
Ngoh Sm fly/ PT
"Ngoh flew (away)"

Table 1: Some Tenses in Nfaw

	IMPERATIVES		PAST TENSE		FUTURE TENSE	
A						
i	pá	"come"	m pil-í	"I came"	ḿ pà	"I will come"
ii	sá	"dance"	n sák-í	"I danced"	ń sá	"I will dance"
iii	bə	"give"	m bək-í	"I gave"	ḿ bə	"I will give"
iv	lá	"tell"	n láb-í	"I beat"	ń lá	"I will beat"
v	Byă	"speak"	m byáb-í	"I spoke"	ḿ byá	"I will speak"
vi	Fá	"put"	m fíl-í	"I put"	ḿ fá	"I will put"
vii	yán	"buy"	n yand-i	"I bought"	ń yan	"I will buy"
viii	wá	"die"	m wúl-i	"I died"	ḿ wa	"I will die"
ix	nyă	"defecate"	nyel-i	"I defecated"	ńya	"I will defecate"
B						
i	búŋgú	"run"	m búŋgú	"I ran"	ḿ búŋgú	"I will run"
ii	pùlú	"climb"	m pulú	"I climbed"	ḿ pulú	"I will climb"
iii	fùmú	"fly"	m fumú	"I flew"	ḿ fumu	"I will fly"
iv	búlú	"kill"	m búlú	"I will kill"	ḿ búlu	"I will kill"
v	fúlú	"wake up"	m fúlú	"I woke up"	ḿ fúlu	"I will wake up"
vi	waŋgú	"shoot"	m waŋgú	"I shot"	ḿ waŋgu	"I will shoot"
C						
i	fyĕlí	"sweep"	m fyĕlí	"I swept"	ḿ fyĕlí	"I will sweep"
ii	məkí	"plait"	m məkí	"I plaited"	ḿ mə	"I will plait"
iii	gbélí	"break"	m gbélí	"I broke sth"	ḿ gbélí	"I will break"
iv	kaní	"think"	ŋ kaní	"I thought"	ŋ´ kani	"I will think"
v	bí	"know"	m bí	"I know"	ḿ bí	"I will know"
vi	nalí	"sleep"	n nalí	"I slept"	ń nalí	"I will sleep"
vii	kúndí	"fall"	ŋ kúndí	"I fell"	ŋ´ kún	"I will fall"
D						
i	samban	"greet"	n sámbán-í	"I greeted"	ń samban	"I will greet"
ii	kwăn	"shake"	ŋ kwăn-í	"I shook"	ŋ´ kwan	"I will shake"
iii	nŭŋ	"take"	n nuŋ-í	"I took"	ń nuŋ	"I will take"
iv	wăn	"fight"	m wan-í	"I fought"	ḿ wan	"I will fight"

v	shúmán "sit"	n shumán-í "I sat"	ń shuman "I will sit"
vi	tíl "write"	n til-í "I wrote"	ń til "I will write"
vii	năn "chase"	n nan-í "I chased"	ń nan "I will chase"
viii	túl "tie"	n túl-í "I tied"	ń tul "I will tie"
ix	wón "plant"	n won-í "I planted"	ń wón "I will plant"
x	pə̀'ŋ "tell"	m pə̀ŋ-í "I told"	ḿ pə̀ŋ "I will tell"
xi	kúm "cook"	ŋ kúm-í "I cooked"	ŋ' kúm "I will cook"

For purposes of comprehension, the table is divided into four parts (A, B, C, & D). It is argued in this study (with evidence from A) that Nfaw has a unique past tense marker – [i]. However, this conclusion is not arrived at straightforwardly. Therefore, Table 1, which comprises some tenses in the language, is intended to lead the reader to a logical conclusion. Whereas the (A) and (D) data clearly exhibit the past tense morpheme, this is not apparent in the (B) and (C) data. The task now is to account for the apparent divergence.

It is largely assumed here that phonology and some historical changes play a crucial role in the forms of Nfaw simple past tense.

As argued in chapter two of this volume, the preferred syllable structure of this language is CV. Like in many other Bantu languages (see Kenstowicz 1994 and Ito 1986) only nasals and liquids are allowed in coda position. It has also been demonstrated that for Grassfields languages (see Hyman and Tadadjeu 1976) that the traditional CVCV verb structure is historically being reduced to a CVC structure with the loss of the final vowel. We argue here that such a historical change is taking place in Nfaw but since only nasals are licensed in the coda position, the resulting final non nasal/liquid consonant is deleted. The result is the CV citation verbs in the imperative forms in A. The data in (B) is peculiar in that it ends in a uniform vowel – [u]. As past tense forms, one would expect to find the tense morpheme suffixed to it, but it is invariably absent. As argued in Tanda and Neba (2006) for Mokpe, another Zone A language, the tense morpheme –i is lost to the rule of V2 deletion discussed in chapter two. This means that the verb roots in B underlyingly end in u and when the suffixal tense marker comes in, it is lost to the rule of vowel deletion.

The same analysis is true for the forms in [C] wherein the verb roots rather end in an -i and the suffixation of the tense marker also results in its deletion. The data in [D] have a straightforward analysis as the predictable past tense marker is quite obvious. In the future tense forms, the past tense –i is absent, evidence that it really marks the past tense. Therefore, the past tense marker is absent in [B] and [C] because of the constraint against two contiguous (high) vowels across morphemes. We therefore conclude that the simple past tense marker is an –i suffixal inflection to the verb root.

4.4.2 The Past Tense and Negation

As we will see in the next chapter, negation in Nfaw is very complex and is better treated as a syntactic phenomenon. However, there is an aspect of it that is expressed as a purely verbal suffix. Given that the past tense marker is also a verbal suffix, it is interesting to describe this morpheme in order to identify the way it interacts with the tense suffix. Table 2 illustrates the negation verbal suffix that we are interested in.

Imperative	Gloss	Past Positive	Gloss	Past negative	Gloss
píjɔ́m	jump	mìmpíjɔ́mí	I jumped	mìmpíjɔ́míjá	I did not jump
díjá	Eat	Mìndílí	I ate	mìndílíjá	I did not eat
pǎ	come	Mìmpílí	I came	mìmpílíjá	I did not come
ʃùmán	Sit	mìʃùmání	I sat	mìʃùmáníjá	I did not sit
púlú	climb	Mìmpúlú	I climbed	mìmpúlúwá	I did not climb
sákí	dance	Mìnsákí	I danced	mìnsákíjá	I did not dance

It can be noticed in the table that when the negative marker is introduced in the past tense form, there is a glide that is inserted after the tense marker and before the negation marker [a].

4.4.3 The Remote Past

This tense is distinguished from the immediate past by adverbials. The type of adverbial determines the degree of remoteness. In essence, adverbials in Nfaw like in many other languages seem to be graded in a way that when native speakers employ them, the extent of remoteness is understood. Consider the following examples.

(12) a. Ngoh a pulú bwə yǎn
Ngoh Sm climb/ PT stick yesterday
"Ngoh climbed a tree yesterday"

b. Ngoh a   gulu   shundí eyɛ   ɛtumbí
   Ngoh Sm   die/ PT Sunday which passed
   "Ngoh died last week"

c. Ngoh a   kumí   lídyǎ ngɔ̌n   eyɛ   ɛtúmbí
   Ngoh Sm   cook/ PT food   month which past
   "Ngoh cooked food last month"

d. Ngoh a   wúní   kaká   mbu   eyɛ   ɛtúmbí
   Ngoh sm   plant/ PT cocoa last year which past
   "Ngoh planted cocoa last year"

e. Ngoh a   búlú   mbul   etún
   Ngoh sm   kill/ PT goat   long time
   "Ngoh killed a goat a long time ago"

Observe that the immediate past form is still attested in all these forms. In other words, the time adverbials are simply adjuncts that can be added to any immediate past tense form. However, an examination of the data in (12) reveals that the adverbials are graded in such a way that the constructions are construed as having either the non-too-distant or remote past reading.

4.4.4 The Non-past Tense
Here, we discuss the present and future tenses in Nfaw.

4.4.5 The Present Tense
There is no tense affix that corresponds to the present moment of speech in Nfaw. The examples we have in Nfaw are ambiguous, as they refer to both actions in progress and in the future. Earlier works on some Bantu languages indicate that this finding is phenomenal (cf Apuge (1998), Ngoisah, (2002:06), Abangma, (2004:115). Consider the following data.

(13) a. Ngoh ǎ   nalí
       Ngoh Sm   sleep/ Tns
       "Ngoh slept/ is sleeping/ will sleep"

b. Ngoh ǎ   búlú   mbul
   Ngoh Sm   kill/ Tns   goat
   Ngoh kills/ is killing/ will kill a goat"

From the data in (13), it is not clear whether the sentences refer to the present progressive or future tenses. However, the position can be disambiguated by the use of an appropriate time adverbial as shown in (14).

(14) a. Ngoh   ǎ   nalí   másonɛ
        Ngoh   sm/ FT   sleep   now
        "Ngoh sleeps/ is sleeping now"

   b. Ngoh   ǎ   nalí   ngə
      Ngoh   Sm/FT   sleep   soon
      "Ngoh will sleep soon"

   c. Ngoh   ǎ   nalí   yán
      Ngoh   Sm/Tns   sleep   tomorrow
      "Ngoh will sleep tomorrow"

Tense in Nfaw can be summarized in the following schemata.

(15) a.   **Tense in Nfaw**

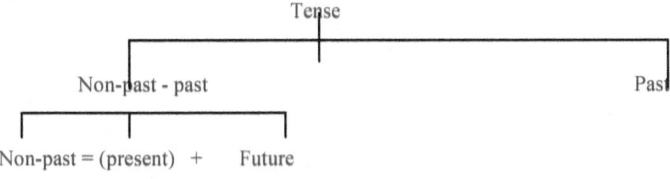

b.   **Tense markers in Nfaw**

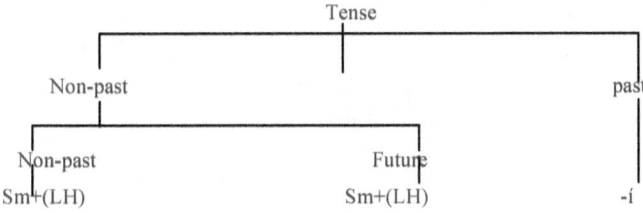

4.5 Aspect in Nfaw

According to Comrie (1976:3) "aspects are different ways of viewing the internal temporal constituency of a situation". Usually, aspectual markers mark the varying facets of an event, or the varying state of affairs as expressed by the situation. In essence, these markers are defined as a set of inflectional forms of the verb that the nature of an action or the manner in which the action is regarded. A major aspectual distinction common in languages of the world is between perfective and imperative (Comrie 1976:25).

In this study, the focus is on three major areas of aspect namely: perfective (PF) or completive aspect, imperfective (IMPF) or incompletive aspect, and habitual aspect.

4.5.1 Perfective/ Completive Aspect

This type of aspect involves lack of explicit reference to the internal temporal constituency of a situation, that is, it indicates the view of a situation as a single whole, without distinction of the various separate phases that make up the situation. The perfective aspect invariably occurs with the past tense. In other words, it cannot occur with the non-past tense. In Nfaw, the perfective marker is **mé**, as shown in (16).

(16) a. Wase a mé nali
   Wase sm/Tns Asp. sleep
   "Wase has slept"

   b. Ngoh a mé wun kaká
   Ngoh Sm/Tns asp plant cocoa
   "Ngoh has planted cocoa"

   c. Ngoh a mé búlú mbúl
   Ngoh Sm/Tns Asp kill goat
   "Ngoh has killed a goat"

   d. Ngoh a mé wan ndzum
   Ngoh Sm/Tns Asp fight fight
   " Ngoh has fought"

4.5.2 Imperfective/Incompletive Aspect
A situation is said to have imperfective meaning if the verbal form makes explicit reference to the internal temporal structures of the situation. In this category, I further dichotomise the present progressive and the past progressive aspects in Nfaw.

4.5.3 The Present Progressive Aspect
The progressive aspect is marked by a rising tone on the subject marker. The examples in (17) bear out this point.

(17) a. Wase ǎ nali
   Wase sm/Asp. sleep
   "Wase is sleeping"

   b. Wase ǎ kúm lídyǎ
   Wase sm/ asp cook food
   "Wase is cooking food"

   e. Ngoh ǎ búlú mbúl
   Ngoh sm/asp kill goat
   "Ngoh is killing a goat"

4.5.4 The Past Progressive Aspect
Unlike the present progressive aspect, this aspect indicates a situation that was on going in the past. It is marked by the morpheme **bílí**. Examples include:

(18) a. Wase a bílí nali
   Wase sm was sleep
   "Wase was sleeping"

   b. Epie a bílí wǎn ndzum
   Epie sm was fight fight
   "Epie was fighting"

   c. Epie a bílí du ɛku
   Epie sm was close door
   "Epie was closing the door"

4.6 Habitual Aspect

This describes a situation that portrays an extended period of time. The period is so intended such that the situation referred to is viewed not as an incidental property of the moment, but precisely, as a characteristic feature of a whole period (reference). In Nfaw, habituality is marked by two verbal prefixes, viz **bílí** and **luŋgú**. Let us consider the following example.

(19) a. Ngoh a bílí adí lá ŋgɔ́m
Ngoh sm/Tns Asp to play drum
"Ngoh used to play drum"

b. Ngoh a luŋgú lá ŋgɔ́m
Ngoh Sm/Tns used to play drum
"Ngoh used to play the drum"

In (19a) the past progressive aspect, **bílí** "was", combines with an infinitive verb **adí** "to play" to express habituality. This phenomenon also obtains in Akoose as argued in Apuge (1998). Consider the following example.

(20) Bé yoke pɔ́n a lím
They used to holes to dig
"They used to dig holes"

In (20b) however, **luŋgú** seems to be an independent morpheme to express habituality. Here, it can be observed that the habitual marker precedes the verb **lá** "to play". The various aspectual markers discussed here are summarized in the following schema.

(21)

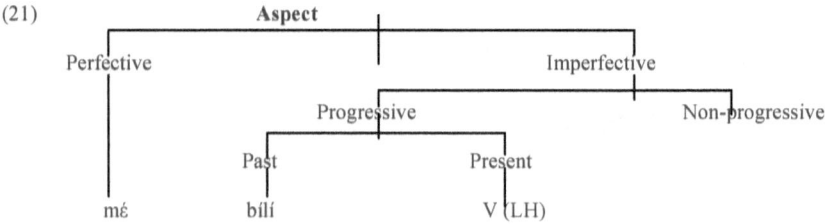

Observe that whereas the perfective and the past progressive aspects are morphologically marked the present progressive is tonal.

4.7 Mood and Modality
Mood also constitutes a verbal category in Nfaw. Ubels (1983: 53) notes that "when there is grammaticalisation of the speaker's opinion of the degree of actuality of a situation, those distinctions are considered to be distinctions of mood". In other words, mood actually states the attitude of a speaker and the degree of his/her belief towards a situation.

Mood is examined as either realis or irrealis mood (Abangma 2004). As shown in the following sub sections, these terms aptly describe the situation in Nfaw.

4.8.1 The Realis Mood
This mood refers to a situation that is asserted as actually taking place or having taken place. According to Payne (1997: 244), "A prototypical realis mood strongly asserts that a specific event or state of affairs has actually happened or actually holds true." A number of scholars have found out that the realis mood corresponds to the indicative mood (Abangma (1985, 1987, 2004), Taylor (1985). Some of the languages studied include Denya, Nkore-kega and Mokpe. In the language under study, this mood is not marked morphologically; rather, it is expressed tonally via the past or progressive tense. Consider the examples below.

(22) a. Epie   à   búlú   mbúl
     Epie   sm   kill/Tns   goat
     "Epie killed a goat"

   b. Epie   ǎ   búlú   mbúl
      Epie sm/ Asp. Kill goat
      "Epie is killing a goat"

The verbs in (22 a-b) can therefore be argued to express the realis mood. In (22a) the act of killing a goat has actually taken place whereas (22b) shows that the action of killing the goat is ongoing. As a result, these situations cannot be denied as they have fully developed at the moment of speaking.

4.8.2 The Irrealis Mood

The irrealis mood unlike the realis mood does not involve the factivity of a situation. This mood is concerned with the potential, contrafactual, possible, hypothetical, dubious and conditional events or actions. A speaker who makes use of the irrealis mood knows indeed that what he/she asserts does not actually hold. This is because whatever is asserted shows a potential for further dynamic development. In this study, the focus is on imperative and deontic/obligational modals.

4.8.3 Deontic/Obligational Modal

Chung and Timberlake (1985) view this mode as one that "Characterises an event as non-actual by virtue of the fact that it is imposed on a given situation". This section is further limited to two sub-types of deontic mode – obligation and permission, as shown in (23) and (24) respectively.

(23) **Obligational Mood**
    a.   N lɔ́lí   ek é skú
        I must go school
        ''I must go to school''

    b.   Bá lɔ́lí kɔ́n mikwɔ́ni míbə
        The must sing songs two
        ''They must sing two songs''

    c.   a   lɔ́lí   ə   wá
        he/she must to die
        ''he/she must to die''

The data in (31) show that the event must hold in all subsequent worlds.

(24) **Permissive Modal**

a. N fítí mwɛ́ màdí?
   I can drink water
   " Can I drink water?"

b. sí fítí wólan?
   We can marry?
   "Can we get married?"

Unlike the obligational mood, the event may be in some subsequent world in the permissive mood.

4.8 Verbal Extensions
In many Bantu languages, the verb is made up of the root and one or more extensions, which add more meaning to the verb stem. These extensions have been referred to as formal affixes (Mutaka and Tamanji (1995).

Extensions examined here include only those that are actually suffixed to the verb. These will include causatives and applicatives.

4.8.1 Causatives
In most cases, the causative has the meaning to cause or to make somebody do something or to cause somebody to become something different. In Nfaw, two morphemes (-á and –ʤí) express causation. Consider the examples below.

(25) a. wan- á   bɔ́ ndzum
       fight caus. them fight
       "Make them fight"

b. nan - ʤí   bɔ́ bá nálí
   sleep caus them pl sleep
   " make them sleep"

c. kɔ́n - á   bɔ́ mi kwɔ́ni
   sing caus them pl song
   "Make them sing songs"

4.8.2 Applicative

Applicative morphemes have the meaning to do something for somebody. The marker in this language is - á. This seems to be the same morpheme for causative. However, for both causatives and applicatives, it is used differently. For causatives, the marker is followed by an objective pronoun that precedes the object noun. Conversely, the lexical object NP follows the applicative marker directly. Note that the examples in these cases take the form of imperatives.

(26) a. wan - á Epie
      fight for Epie
      '' fight for Epie''

   b. kɔn - á   Ngoh
      Sing for Ngoh
      '' Sing for Ngoh''

   c. kání - á Wase
      pray for Wase
      ''pray for Wase''

4.9 Summary and Conclusion

The goal in this chapter has been to present a description of the Nfaw verbal category. In essence, verb classes and their classification, tone, syllable and verb structure on the one hand, and tense, aspect and mood (TAM) on the other hand have been examined. In addition, (suffixal) verbal extensions, mainly causatives and applicatives have been discussed.

   This analysis has revealed that Nfaw makes use of tense aspect and mood. Generally, the language displays the following verb structure: TNS+ NEG + ROOT, TNS + ASP + ROOT, ROOT + SUFFIX (causative or applicative). Tense distinctions noted in the study are: past, present, and future. However, these distinctions can further be subsumed under past and non-past tense categories. Whereas the past tense is construed as immediate and remote past (labeled P1 and P2 respectively), the non-past tense is understood as either the present or future tense. Note that while the past (both immediate and remote past) is marked by a low tone on the subject marker, the non-past (present and future) is marked by a rising tone on the subject marker. This is precisely because the non-past in Nfaw is ambiguous; referring to the present on the one hand and both actions in progress and in the future on the other; it even refers to habitual events.

Mood and aspect are also grammaticalised in the language. In this study, aspect has broadly been examined under the perfective, imperfective and habitual distinctions, with the imperfective further subdividing into progressive and non-progressive. The past progressive and the present progressive are subheadings of the progressive aspect that this work treats. Under the mood category, two broad distinctions are considered, namely the realis and irrealis mood. Concretely however, this study focuses only on imperative and deontic/obligational modal.

Another interesting verbal satellite that has been examined in this work is verbal extensions. The productive verbal extensions attested in the language are causatives and applicatives. These have an important semantic role in that the meaning of the verb is extended from an ordinary to a specific reading/interpretation.

Concretely therefore, this study has presented a description of Nfaw verbal category. The elements of verb structure, tense, aspect, mood and verbal extensions have been shown, how they distribute and what role they play in Nfaw morphology. It will be interesting to see how this research domain can be accounted for within a particular linguistic formalism in the language under study.

Notes

1. The low tone is not marked in this study (except in otherwise stated cases for purposes of clarity).

References

Abangma, S.N. (1985) The Interrelation between Aspect and mood in Denya, *JWAL*.15.2 pp110- 122.

Abangma, S.N. (1987) *Modes in Denya Discourse*. Dallas: Summer Institute of Linguistics and the University of Texas at Arlington.

Abangma, S.N. (2004) *Descriptive Studies of Mokpe*. Design House Limbe.

Apuge, M. E. (1998) On Operator Construction in Akoose Syntax. MA thesis, university of Buea.

Asongwed, T. and L. Hyman. (1976). Morphotonology of the Ngamabo Noun. In Larry M. Hyman (ed.), *Studies in Bantu Tonology*. (Southern California Occasional papers in Linguistics) Los Angeles: University of Southern California, pp. 23-56.

Bearth, T. (2003). Syntax, in Bantu, D. Nurse & G. Philippson (eds.), London: Routledge. 121-42.

Comrie, B. (1976) *Aspect*. Cambridge, Cambridge University Press.

Chia, E.N. (1976) Tense and Aspect in Kom, Ph D. Thesis: George Town University, Washington.

Chung and Timber L. A. (1985) Tense, Aspect, Mood in Timothy Shopen ed. *Language Typology and Syntactic Description* Vol. III Grammatical Categories. PP. 201-258. Cambridge, Cambridge University Press.

Hedinger (2004). A Grammar of Akoose. SIL Cameroon.

Hyman, Larry and Maurice Tadadjeu (1976). Floating tones in Mbam-Nkam. In Larry M. Hyman (ed.), *Studies in Bantu tonology*. (Southern California Occasional papers in Linguistics) Los Angeles: University of Southern California, pp. 57-111.

Itō, Junko. (1986). *Syllable theory in prosodic phonology*. Ph.D. dissertation. Massachusetts Institute of Technology, Cambridge.

Kenstowicz, Michael. (1994). *Phonology in generative grammar.* Cambridge: Blackwell.

Leroy, J. (1979) 'A la recherche de tons perdus: structure tonale du nom en ngemba' *Journal of African Languages and Linguistics.* 1 pp 55-71.

Meeussen, A. E. (1967) *Bantu Grammatical Reconstructions.* Africana Linguistica. Vol. 3.

Mfonyam, J. N. (1989). *Tone in Orthography: the case of Bafut and related languages.* A Doctorat D'Etat Thesis. University of Yaounde.

Mutaka, P. N. (1994). *The lexical tonology of Kinande,* Munchen: Lincom Europa.

Mutaka, N.M. and P. N. Tamanji (2000). An introduction to African linguistics. Ms Université Catholique de l'Afrique Centrale/I.C.Y and University of Yaounde I Published in 2000.

Tanda, V. A. and **Ayu'nwi N. Neba.** (2005). Negation in Mokpe and Two Related Coastal Bantu Languages of Cameroon. African Study Monographs, Vol. 26, No. 4. 201-219.

Ngoisah, F.M (2002) The Morphology of The Noun Phrase and the Verb Phrase in Mokpe in Relation to Orthography. M.A. Dissertation, University of Buea.

Nurse, D. (2003). Tense and Aspect in Bantu Languages, in Bantu, D. Nurse & Philippson (eds). 90-102. London: Routledge.

Payne, T. E. (1997) *Describing Morpho-Syntax: A Guide for field Linguistics.* Cambridge, Cambridge University Press.

Pike, K. (1948) *Tone Languages.* University of Michigan Press. Ann Arbor.
Schadeberg (2003) Derivation, in Bantu, D. Nurse & Philippson (eds). 71-89. London: Routledge.

Tallerman Maggie (1998). *Understanding Syntax.* New York: Oxford University Press.

Taylor, C (1985) *Nkore-Kiga*, London, Croom Hem.

Ubels, E.H. (1983) *African Languages Structure*. Berkeley, University of California Press.

Welmers, W. E. (1973) *African Language Structures*. Berkeley: University of California Press.

Yule, G. (1996) *The Study of Language* Cambridge: CUP.

Chapter Five

The Syntax of Nfaw

Vincent A. Tanda

5.0 Introduction

Syntax is the branch of language study that focuses on the combinatorial possibilities of the words of a language to form larger constituents such as phrases, clauses and sentences, which convey meaning and communicate messages. The way words are allowed to co-occur in larger grammatical constituents such as clauses and sentences is licensed by features which are inherent in each word, and these words by and large, are categorized into 9 classes. It is not all of the world's languages that make use of all these classes. Within a grammatical phrase or clause, the words of such constituents usually have a fixed linear order. In no language of the world are words allowed to appear just anywhere and anyhow within a grammatical constituent. Each word has a recognized position within a grammatical sentence, and even though languages are productive in the sense that their users have the freedom to create novel sentences whenever they want to convey some new information and to move certain word classes from one position to another, that freedom operates within this framework of syntax.

On the basis of observable data, linguists posit that the words of a language may be grouped into various categories. Some categories are considered major and others minor. The assumption in linguistics is that words of the major categories combine in various patterns to form phrases, clauses and sentences. Words of the major categories, usually considered heads, combine with those of the minor categories, serving as modifiers, or complements.

Each language has a basic word order. Sentences which follow the basic word order of a language constitute the core (or kernel) sentences from which are derived other sentence types. From this basic sentence type, other sentence types are derived either by reversing word order, moving, deleting or adding some other elements to achieve interrogative, imperative, exclamatory, focus sentences, etc.

The present chapter is concerned with the Syntax of Nfaw. Syntax is a broad area of language study, which includes the various structures of grammatical sentences and it is impossible to cover every aspect of it in a document as this one. This chapter therefore is only an overview of the Syntax of the language and covers, cursorily, various aspects of Nfaw syntax. The main focus is on the description of two aspects of Nfaw syntax: interrogatives and negatives.

5.1 Word Categories

As we observed above, words are the building blocks of sentences, and sentences make up a language. It is obvious, therefore, that we begin the discussion in this chapter with lexical categories. Nfaw makes use of four major categories: nouns, verbs, adjectives, and prepositions and five minor categories: pronouns, determiners, conjunctions, intensifiers and interjections.

Given the frequency of use, nouns and verbs will be observed to be very important lexical categories in Nfaw. We will illustrate each of these categories as the discussion develops.

5.1.1 The Basic Word Order and Sentence Structure of Nfaw
The basic word order of Nfaw is Subject (S) Verb (V)[1] object (O) - SVO. By studying sentences in the language which are declarative, affirmative and active containing a transitive verb, and which have noun phrases functioning as S and O, we come to the conclusion that the SVO structure is the basic word order in the language. Let us consider the following sentences:

(1.) Njume à kwĕ Mary
   Njume SM hate mary
   "Njume hates mary".

(2.) Peter à abílí idíá màʃă
   Peter SM prog pst eat plums
   "Peter was eating plums".

Notice that the S is followed by an agreement word or subject marker (SM), the V and then O. In the case where the verb is intransitive there is no O.

5.1.2. Subject and Predicate Agreement

Just like the agreement between a noun and its dependents discussed in chapter three, there is an agreement between the subject noun phrase and the predicate within the sentence. This cross-referencing is signaled by a verb prefix. This is exemplified in (3a) where we have the prefix *si-* in the verb which agrees in number and class with the subject noun phrase. In this language the subject noun phrase may be omitted. However, the verbal prefix must be present, as in (3b). In this case the verbal prefix functions as an affixed or dependent subject pronoun.

(3a) sɛ sí-kùlù?
    we AGR-sick
    "We are sick".

(3b) sí-kùlù?
    AGR-sick
    "We are sick".

There is no evidence of any agreement between the verb and object NP.

5.2. Mood and Sentence Structure

Four moods are generally identified to constitute sentence types in any language. The indicative mood characterizes declarative sentences, which involves situations presented as facts through the use of statements or assertions. The imperative and the interrogative moods present commands and questions respectively while the subjunctive mood expresses wishes, possibilities or uncertainty. Some of these moods and their morphology have been discussed in chapter four. In this section, we lay emphasis on syntactically relevant issues.

5.2.1 The Imperative Mood

In the imperative mood, the speaker commands or gives an order to a listener to act accordingly. the syntactically relevant point to note here is the fact that the subject noun phrase is omitted in the imperative, leaving the sentence with only the verb or verb and object as shown in (4) and (5).

(4) ké á ndùkú
   go to farm
   "go to the farm!"

(5) diá? lidiá?   Eat food
   "Eat some food!"

As demonstrated in chapter four, the imperative in this language is marked with an H tone on the last syllable of the verb.

5.2.2 The Interrogative Mood
Interrogative sentences generally serve to elicit information from an interlocutor. Because of the nature of responses that are different, interrogatives are referred to variously. The response could be in the form of yes/no (as in English) in which case they are referred to as yes/no questions, as in the following example:

(6) é wəlí ?
   you marry
   "Are you married?"

It is note worthy here that in Nfaw what marks Yes/No questions is a rising intonation. The answer to such questions in Nfaw is either: é "yes", or ai "no". The tag-question takes the form of a statement followed by the question tag sàkà nâ ("isn't it"), as exemplified below.

(7) bá búmúp, sàkà nâ?
   They mad   not   so
   "They are mad, aren't they?"

Interrogative sentences may also be formed by the use of a question word (Wh- word in English) such as ndʒá (what, which, who), ɣə (why), and əfə ('which'), as in the following sentence.

(8) ndʒá wĕ dia-ni?
   What you eat- ext²
   "What are you eating?"

In the following section, we discuss question word types.

5.3 Wh-operators and Question Formation
Interrogative operators are used in a sentence as question particles to elicit information. Since such operators are typically Wh-words in English, they are commonly referred to in the literature as Wh-operators. We use the term Wh-operator here as a convenient equivalent for "interrogative operator", because Nfaw Wh-operators do not have the Wh-form. There is a considerable degree of difference as shown in table I.

Table I

Nfaw	English
ndʒá	what, which, who, how
yə	how, why, what
əfə	Which

(9) ndʒá dĭdə wə idí ni?
   What name of you is
   "what is your name?"

10) a) yə bə bábá ɛ́túm ?
   Why they cross road
   "why did they cross the road?"

11) yə idí bumbú jə?
   what is   day   today
   "what is the day of today?"

12) yə bànbán bá bəni?
   How children SM do
   "How are the children doing?"

Section 3.3.1 below presents a brief description of each of these operators.

5.3.1 Typology of Wh-Operators
Wh-operators fall in two categories: arguments, and adjuncts. Adjuncts could further be sub-classified as referential or non-referential (Noun 1986). In this section, we describe each Wh-operator, its logical position, state whether it moves or not, and its landing site where movement applies. Table II below summarises the

distribution of Nfaw operators as arguments and adjuncts. The use of the terms argument and adjunct here refers to the grammatical role that the phrases play in the sentence.

Table 2

Arguments	Adjuncts	
	Referential	Non-Referential
ndʒá "who", "what"	fɛ̀ "where"	ján "how"
ɛndʒá "whose"	ndʒá púnda "when"	jɛ̀ "why"
		étín "how much / how many"

It can be observed that there is considerable semantic overlap. This implies that the same operator could potentially behave like an argument or an adjunct depending on the context in which it is used.

5.3.1.1 Argument Operators
ndʒá (what, which, who).
ndʒá in Nfaw functions both as a determiner and a pronoun. As a determiner, it modifies head nouns as in (20) below, and both elements function as the object of the transitive verb, in either sentential positions.

13) a) wə bwɛ̀ lání ndʒá kó?   b) ndʒá kó wə bwɛ̀ lání?
   You prog use   which cup   Which cup you prog use
   "You are using which cup?"   "Which cup are you using?"

In (13a), the NP ndʒá kó is in situ, while in (13b) it is moved or fronted. In Nfaw, however, this movement is not accompanied by NP-Aux inversion. Exploiting the strength metaphor that has been developed by Chomsky, the Q – affix (question affix, which fills head C position in questions) has weak features, hence there is no motivation for Aux to adjoin to it. Of course, this would be understood as one of the lines along which there is parametric variation between Languages (±Strong Q-affix). Accordingly, while English selects [+strong], Nfaw selects [-strong].

As in Standard English, the constraint on preposition stranding necessitates the movement of a whole PP which contains the operator as in (14) below.

14) a) ə fóné lífù á ndʒá kó ?
   You pour oil in which cup
   "You poured the oil in which cup?"

b) á ndʒá kó wè fóné lífù
   In which cup you pour oil
   "In which cup did you pour the oil?"

As a personal pronoun, ndʒá ('who') may be used as subject or complement of a verb. In subject position, the expression containing ndʒá is base generated. (15) and (16) below exemplify this.

15) a) ndʒá ă kə̀ ?
   "Who will go?"

b) ndʒá mɛ́nɛ́ mɔ?
   who see him
   "Who saw him?"

16) a) nă á tó nà ndʒá
   Mother SM talk with who
   "Mother is talking with who?"

jə̀ (what, how, why)

This morpheme functions both as an argument and a non referential adjunct. jə̀ ('what'), is used to question constituents and in this case, it functions as an argument. Used as an argument, it is subject to movement as shown in (17) and (18).

17) a) wə sɔ̀ní jə̀
   you want what
   "You want what?"

b) jə̀ wə sɔ̀ní
   what you want
   "What do you want?"

18) a) mó à dʒìbijə̀?
She SM steal what
"She has stolen what?"

b) jə̀ mó à dʒìbi
what she SM steal
"what has she stolen"

It can also be used to seek information about circumstances such as the well-being of an individual. This is its use as a non referential adjunct, exemplified in (19-20) below. Note however that *jə̀* ('how') may only be employed s-initially in this language but not s-finally. This is shown by the ungrammaticality of (19).

19) *wə βwə̀ní jə̀?
you do how
"You are doing how?"

20)   jə̀ wə βwə̀ní?
how you do
"How are you doing?"

It is noteworthy that the use of *jə̀* is limited to situations when the speaker directly seeks information about the hearer. Where a speaker asks about some other person (for example the hearer's children), the operator used is *ján* ('how'). As a non referential adjunct, *jə̀* is used to question why things happen, as in (21) and (22).

21) a) mwăn ă dʒì jə̀ ?
Child SM cry why?
"The child will cry why?"

b) jə̀ mwăn ă dʒìni?
why child SM cry
"Why will the child cry?"

22) a) wə dʒwìní jó jè
      You kill   it why
      "You are killing it why?"

  b) jè wə dʒwìní jó?
      why you kill   it
      "Why are you killing it?"

In both cases, there is movement of the operator to the pre-subject position.

jè, followed by the verb *bwèlí* ("happen") is also used to mean "why" as in the following example:

23) jè bwèlí kən nʒium ɛbà?
    What happen that fight occur.
    "Why was there a fight?"

In such constructions, the logical position of the operator is the sentence initial position as can be demonstrated by the ungrammaticality of (24).

24) *kən nʒium ɛbà jè bwèlí? .
    That fight   occur what happen
    "Why was there a fight?"

A similar instance where jè occurs only sentence initially is in constructions that end in a predicative adjective such as (25) and (26) below.

25) a) jè bɔ̀ bə wóní mújón?
      Why Foc they feel ashamed
      "Why will they feel ashamed?"

  b) * bɔ̀ bə wóní mújón jè?
      Foc they feel ashamed why?
      "Why will they feel ashamed?"

26) a) jè mwàlán nə á jabíni?
    Why woman that SM tall
    "Why is that woman tall?"

b) * mwàlán nə á jabíni jè
    woman that SM tall why?

Here again, the operator must move to the pre-subject position for the sentence to be grammatical.

éfé (which)
This operator is used in questions which entail making a choice between two or more things. In sentences where the questioned object is named, **éfé** can either occur in its logical position, or be moved and fronted as in (27) and (28).

27) ndáp éfé wə nɨɲíní
    House which you like
    "Which house do you like?"

28) a) wə é kóní ŋkóni éfé
    You SM sing song which
    "Which song are you singing?"

b) ŋkóni éfé wə é kóní
    song which you sing
    "Which song are you singing?"

Alternatively, in questions which do not name the questioned object, movement is obligatory. This is exemplified in (29).

29) a) éfé wə nɨɲíní ?
     Which you SM you like
     "Which do you like?"

b) * wə é nɨɲíní éfé?
   You SM like which

Such questions are typically used in contexts where the questioned objects have been named in preceding utterances, such that knowledge of what is questioned is presupposed.

ɛndʒá *(whose)*

ɛndʒá ('whose') is used as a determiner in nominal constructions to indicate possession. When the phrase containing it is in object position, it can be moved and fronted. (30) and (31) below show this.

30) a) wə bwèlání ɛfiàŋ ɛndʒá?
       You use   broom   whose
       "You are using whose broom?"

   b) ɛfiàŋ ɛndʒá wə bwèláni?
      broom whose you use
      "Whose broom are you using?"

31) a) wə mɛnɛ mò á túŋ ɛndʒá?
       You saw him in room whose
       "You saw him in whose room?"

   b) á túŋ ɛndʒá wə mɛnɛ mò?
      in room whose you saw him
      "In whose room did you see him?"

5.3.1.2 *Referential Adjuncts*

In our discussion of argument operators above we made sporadic reference to adjuncts. In this section, we give a description of operators which function as referential adjuncts.

fé *(where)*

This operator is used to question location as in (23).

32) a) bèbòŋ bé di fé?

Chairs SM are where
"The chairs are where?"

b) **fé bèbòŋ bé di-ni?**
Where chairs SM are
"Where are the chairs?"

fé could also be used to mean "which". In this case, it is an argument as in (24)

33) a) **fésé ă lá? mwăn fé?**
Fese SM beat child which
"Fese will beat which child?"

b) mwăn **fe fésé** mɔ ă lá?ni?
child which Fese Foc SM beat
"Which child will Fese beat?"

c)* mwăn **fe** Fese mɔ ă lá?ni?
child which Fese foc SM beat
"Which child will Fese beat?"

It would be noted here that fronting **fe** necessitates the introduction of a focus element (32b), and that the absence of this element results in ungrammaticality (32c).

ndʒá Púndá (when)

This is a compound word composed of ndʒá (what), and Púndá (time). As an adverbial adjunct, its logical position in a sentence is post verbal. However, as (33d) and (34) below show, it must move to pre-subject position for the sentence to be grammatical.

33d) ndʒá púndá ngàndù abutàní?
What time feast start
"When will the feast start?"

34) ndʒá púndá wə bíní mbíà?
   What time you were talk
   "When were you talking?"

But when the operator is preceded by a preposition, movement is optional and the sentence is grammatical when it is in situ. (35) illustrates this.

35) a) wə nòní mary à ndʒá púndá?
   you see Mary at what time
   "You saw Mary at what time?"

   b) à ndʒá púnda wə nòní mary?
   at what time you see Mary.
   "At what time did you see Mary?"

5.3.1.3 Non Referential Adjuncts
ján ('How', 'what')
   When translated as "how", *ján* is an operator used in seeking information about circumstances, as in (36).

36) a) ngàndù nə̀ ə̀díni ján?
   feast that was how
   "The feast was how?"

   b) ján ngàndù nə̀ ə̀díni?
   How feast that was
   "How was the feast?"

Ján is also used when demanding the price of something. In this use, ŋkùn ("price") is followed by a focus marker as shown below:

37) a) ŋkùn mɔ ə̀díni ján?
   Price foc is   how
   "Its price is how much?"

   b) ján ŋkùn mɔ ə̀díni?
   how price foc is
   "How much is its price?"

When *ján* is used to ask someone's name or to seek information about something belonging to someone, it can be translated as "what"; used in this way, it is an argument and can be fronted as in (38) below.

38) a) dĭndé wè idí ni ján?
   Name of you is what
   "Your name is what?"

It may also precede a preposition in expressions like *ján ná* (what of) as in (46).

39) ján ná búmbú nî?
   what of your name is "Your name is what?"

étíŋ (how much, how many)
   This non referential adjunct is an operator used in making enquiries about number and amount. In (40) below, it is used to question number, while in (41) it questions amount.

40) a) cletus à ʃúmé mbwá étɪŋ?
   Cletus SM sell dogs how much?
   "Cletus sold how many dogs?"

   b) mbwá étɪŋ cletus à ʃúméni?
   dogs how many Cletus SM sell
   "How many dogs did Cletus sell?"

41) a) è jàndí jó kápè étɪŋ?
   You buy it money how much
   "You bought it for how much?"

   b) kápe étɪŋ è jàndí jó?
   money how much you buy it
   "How much did you buy it?"

This operator generally agrees with the noun it precedes. In (42) below for example, it takes the *ma*-prefix of *ma-lɛ* (stones), while in (42) it takes *bi-* of *bi-ngà* (cows).

42) peter à pè màlɛ́ métɨŋ?
Peter SM carry stones how many?
"Peter carried how many stones?"

43) móʔ ngà a mbòló bìŋgà bitɨŋ?
Man cow SM kill cows how many
"The Butcher killed how many cows?"

3.3.2 The Role of WH-Operators in Questioning Constituents

One of the main features of a Wh-question is that it contains a questioned constituent. Following Bambose (1974), Wh-operators generally question the noun(s) or the verb in a sentence. In this section, we examine in turn, the role of Nfaw Wh-operators in questioning NPs and VPs. Consider the exchange in (44).

44) a) ndʒá à dʒwǐ nɔ̀?
Who SM kill cow
"Who killed the cow?"

b) Ekoko à dʒwǐ nɔ̀.
"Ekoko killed the cow."

It is obvious that the questioned NP in (44a) is the subject, which is supplied in the response in (44b). Alternatively, a truncated response "Ekoko" would still be appropriate. When the questioned NPs are characterised in terms of the feature [± human], the operators used are *ndʒá* ('who') and *jə̀* ('what'). Consider now the examples in (45a) and (46a), and the responses in (45b and 46b).

45 a) ndʒá dʒíbí ŋgwì?
   Who steal pig
   "Who stole the pig?"

b) ndʒib nè̩ mɔ̀ á dʒíbí ŋgwì
   Thief that Foc SM stole pig
   "The chief (himself) stole the pig."

46) a) jə ndʒib nə á dʒíbí ni?
   What that that SM steal
   "What has the thief stolen?"

b) ndʒib nè̩ á dʒíbí ngwì.
   Thief that SM steal pig
   "The thief stole the pig."

While in (45) the questioned constituent is the subject, the questioned constituent in (46) is the object.

So far, we have characterised questioned NPs along lines of [± human] such that [+ human] nouns are questioned with ndʒá *('who')*, and [- human] with jə ('what'). This categorisation is however inadequate in examples like (47) below.

47) a) jə mùd nè̩ dí?
   What man that is
   "That man is what?"

b) mùd nè̩ dí ndʒíb?
   Man that is thief
   "That man is a thief?"

In (47b) *ndʒíb* (thief) which is [± human] occurs in response to the operator *jə* (what), which is used for [- human] nouns. This suggests that the dichotomy human versus non human is inadequate to characterise the questioned constituents. In 47b), the hearer is concerned with providing a general identification or label for mud ('man') which places him in a given category. If we characterise this categorisation in terms of the semantic features [± attributes], (Bambose 1974:6), we could say that any noun that has the features [+human, + attributive] will be questioned by jǝ (what).

It could be observed that sentences like (46) with attributive NPs can be traced to basic non topicalised sentences like (48).

48) a) mùd nə̀ à dî ndʒíb.
    Man that SM is thief
    "That man is a thief."

b) nsum mia à dî cláki.
    friend my SM is Clerk
    "My friend is a Clerk

Operators could also be used to elicit information about an action or a state. In this case, the questioned constituent is the VP as in (49) and 50) below.

49) a) jǝ fese mɔ̀ βwè ní?
    What Fese Foc do
    "What did Fese do?"

b) Fese à ʃùm mábàd
    Fese SM sell dresses
    "Fese sold dresses."

50) a) jǝ Fese á díní?
    What Fese is like
    "What is Fese like?"

b) Fese à jàbí
    Fese SM tall.
    "Fese is tall"

The response in (49b) describes an action while (50b) describes a state.

Following Bambose (1974), verbs could be divided into four semantic types: action, occurrence, quality, and experience. In Nfaw, an action can be questioned with *jə* "what". (51 a, b and c) are thus appropriate answers to (41a) above.

51 a) fese à ké.
   Fese SM go
   "Fese went."

  b) fese à tăti makolo.
   Fese SM look Mokolo
   "Fese looked at Makolo."

  c) fese à bwɛlí nsám
   Fese SM do something
   "Fese did something

A verb of occurrence expresses a change of state which could be physical or emotional. In Nfaw, such verbs can be questioned with *jə*. Consider (52) below.

52) a) ɛkìí íbwélí.
   "egg broke"
   "The egg broke."

  b) mwăn nò à kùndú.
   child that SM fell
   "The child fell."

  c) ndʒɛ ɛ wà? bɔ́ ?
   hunger is hurt them
   "They are hungry."

Though both action and occurrence verbs are questioned with the operator jə, the appropriate question in the latter case is jə bwɛlí (what happened?). Of course, it would be odd to say jə ɛkìlí mɔ bwɛní (what did the egg do?). In questioning a verb of quality, it is inappropriate to ask what the subject is doing or what happened to it.

In summary, this section we have examined the structure of interrogatives in Nfaw. On the whole, Nfaw, just like English, employs Yes-No questions, Wh-questions, and tag questions. It has been observed that Nfaw has a more restricted set of Wh-operators, hence the same operator in Nfaw could be translated variously in English depending on the context of use. Finally, it has been noted that these operators function differently in questioning different constituents.

5.4 Negation

Negation is a process whereby a negative particle is added to a sentence or constituent expressing a proposition with the intention of reversing the truth condition of that proposition. Over the years, negation has constituted a major domain of research within descriptive, typological, and theoretical linguistics. According to Trask (1993), the expression of negation has been observed to vary widely among languages in the sense that while some languages will ubiquitously employ a single morpheme invariably to mark negation, some others employ more than one morpheme. For instance, while the English language uses *not* to mark negation, other languages such as Mokpe (Lyonga 2002), Nfaw, etc employ not less than three. Bafut uses the discontinuous morpheme *kaa...sî* (Chumbow and Tamanji 1994). The question to answer here is why some languages like English and French make use of the morphemes *not* and *ne pas* respectively invariably, while some others like Nfaw use three or more to achieve the same purpose.

Furthermore, in some of the world's languages the negation marker is preverbal and in others it occurs at the end of the sentence (see Mendandi (2003) and others). Interestingly as well, although the negation marker is a free morpheme in a language like English, in Efik (Mensah 2001) it is a bound morpheme attached to the verb. This section seeks to investigate the structure of negative constructions in

Nfaw. Nfaw employs the following negative morphemes: ʃɛ̌, áwə, òsì, á?, sǎ, sî, káká and ká. ʃɛ̌, òsì, sǎ, sî, káká and ká, **usually recede the verb in a sentence while** áwə **and** á? **occur at the postverbal position. Consider the following Nfaw sentences which have been presented earlier:**

(53a) à nùŋ mákánì
    he say prayer
    'He is praying.'

(b) à ʃɛ̌ nùŋ mákánì
    he Neg say prayer
    'He is not praying.'

(54a) mì mɛ̀ nálí?
    I P1 sleep
    'I have slept.'

(b) mì nálì? áwə
    I sleep Neg
    'I have not slept.'

Note that in (53b) the negation morpheme ʃɛ̌ precedes the verb, but in (54b) the morpheme áwə comes after the verb. Our objective in this work is to present a description of the phenomenon of negation in Nfaw. The results attained here will add to the literature on negation in the World's languages. This work is divided into two main parts. The first part handles the relationship between negation and tense, while the second section examines negation in relation to sentence structure.

5.4.1 Tense and Negation

In Nfaw, like related Coastal Bantu languages, negation is intricately linked to tense such that the negative particle used varies with respect to the tense of the verb. This treatment therefore links negation with tense. Tense relates the time of occurrence of an action, event or state to the time when it is described. It could be marked morphologically by inflections on the verb or by an auxiliary as in English, or syntactically by free tense morphemes in a sentence. Often, as is the case in declarative sentences in Nfaw, on introduction of the aspectual marker ə̀, tense is realized as a tonal morpheme on the negative particle. In the following section, we examine the syntax of negation in Nfaw.

5.4.1.1 The Present Tense

The present tense is generally used to describe events occurring at the time of description, but could also be used for habitual events. In Nfaw, this tense is unmarked morphologically. We want to note however, that unlike in many Bantu languages where this tense is marked by a tonal morpheme, the Nfaw data do not seem to bear this out. Consider the following examples:

(55a) mì dí á ndáp
    I   be   in   house
    'I am in the house.'

(b) mì ʃɛ̆ á ndáp
    I   Neg   in   house
   'I am not in the house.'

(56a) à nùŋ mákànì
      he say prayer
      'He is praying.'

(b) à   ʃɛ̆ nùŋ mákànì
    he Neg say prayer
    'He is not praying.'

The corresponding negative particle for the present tense is ʃɛ̌. The sentences in (55a) and (56a) are negated as in (55b) and (56b). The negative form of (55b) shows that with the addition of the negative particle ʃɛ̌, the verb dí ('be') as in (55a) is omitted. If the meaning of the sentence can be deduced in the absence of the verb, then one can stipulate that the negative particle has qualities which facilitate this interpretation. Tanda and Neba (2006) observe that in Mokpe, a neighbouring coastal Bantu language of Cameroon, negation relates to tense such that the negative marker completely replaces the tense morpheme. For such omission to be possible, the condition of recoverability must be met. In this case, since negative morphemes are tagged to tenses, the tense of a sentence could be deduced from the negative morpheme used. Thus, in these languages, functional categories can be replaced by the negative particle. In fact, Mokpe displays a similar correlation between tense and negation though it employs fewer morphemes. The following Mokpe examples would illustrate this.

(57a) á má βándʒà
he past jump
'He jumped.'

(b) à zrí βándʒà
he Neg jump
'He did not jump.'

(58a) à wélìlí βándʒà
he Prog jump
'He is jumping.'

(b) à zrá βàndʒá
he Neg jump
'He is not jumping.'

Both examples above show that the tense morpheme is dropped in the negative sentence. Returning to the Nfaw example, the omission of 'to be' is possible because it lacks semantic content. This explains why verbs with semantic content cannot be omitted in this way.

5.4.1.2 The Past Tense
This tense is used to describe events / actions that took place prior to the time of description. Like most Bantu languages, Nfaw has various past tenses which describe the degree of remoteness (in time) of an event from the time of description. Three of these tenses are discussed here: the immediate past, the non-too-distant past, and the remote past.

5.4.1.2.1 The Immediate Past
The immediate past focuses on "just completed" actions. To negate sentences in the immediate past, the particles *áwə* and *áʔ* are employed as in 59 -60 below.

(59a) mì mɛ̀ nálíʔ
    I P1 sleep
    'I have slept.'

(b) mì mɛ̀ nálìʔ áwə
    I P1 sleep Neg
    'I have not slept.'

(60a) à mɛ̀ kú bɜ̀dʒì.
    he P1 stop crying
    'He has stopped crying.'

(b) à mɛ̀ kú áwə bɜ̀dʒì
    he P1 stop Neg cry
    'He has not stopped crying.'

(61a) ekoko à mɛ̀ kúndí.
    Ekoko SM P1 fail
    'Ekoko has failed.'

(b)   Ekoko à mɛ̀ kúndì á?.
      Ekoko SM P1 fail Neg
      'Ekoko has not failed.'

(62) * mì mɛ̀ nálì? ʃɛ̆.
      I   P1   sleep Neg
      'I have not slept.'

The (b) sentences are the corresponding negative forms of those in (a). It should be observed here that *áwə* and *à?* occur in free variation. Where one appears, it is possible to replace it with the other without any alteration in meaning. However, in this tense *ʃɛ̆* is unacceptable as shown by the ungrammaticality of (63).

The lowering of the second high tone on the verb stems *kúndí* and *nálí?* in (59b) and (62b) on addition of the negative particle is probably a reflex of Stevick's rule which delinks the second branch of a high tone when it is followed by another at word boundary. According to Mutaka and Tamanji (2000) the low tone on these vowels is ultimately assigned by default.

5.4.1.2.2 The Non-Too-Distant Past (P2)
This tense is distinguished from the immediate past by adverbials such as *wújə* ('this morning') and *mbù mɛ ntúmbi* ('last month'). The negative marker for this tense is *á?* as in (63) and (64).

(63a) sî   bî   sā?   məsákì   wú   jə.
       we were dance dance morning   this
       'We were dancing this morning.'

(b)   sî   bílì   á? ésá? məsákì   wu   jə
       we were Neg dance dance morning this
       'We were not dancing this morning.'

(64a) à dʒǐ a mbú mɛ ntúmbi.
   she cry Prep month which passed
   'She cried last month.'

(b) à bíli áʔ dzǐ mbú mɛ ntúmbi.
   she was Neg cry month which passed
   'She did not cry last month.'

Apparently, there is no P2 marker. However, given that low melody verb roots like *dʒǐ* ('cry') take a rising tone in this tense, it is logical to posit that this tense is marked by a floating high tone. This tonal morpheme links to low melody roots yielding the attested LH. The high tone linking applies vacuously to high melody roots like *diáʔ* ('eat') so that the phonetic form does not change. When the negative morpheme is introduced as in (63b) and (64b) above, the full forms of *bî* and *sǎ* are used. However, though the positive forms are truncated, the tones are not affected. Thus *bî* and *sǎ* have HL (falling) and LH (rising) tones respectively which are the same melodies in the full forms *bílì* (HL) and *èsáʔ* (LH).

5.4.1.2.3 The Remote Past (P3)
The remote past tense as the name implies describes events which occurred in the distant past. It bears similarity to the non-too-distant past, the two being set apart by the time adverials used such as a long time ago, etc. Like in the non-distant past, the negative morpheme is *áʔ* as in (65) and (66).

(65a) mi bî á wə á púndɛ nì.
   I was Loc there at time that
   'I was there at that time.'

(b) mi bílì áʔ á wə á púndɛ nì
   I was Neg Loc there at time that
   'I was not there at that time.'

(66a) mì ndílí garri púndɛ nì
       I eat garri time that
       'I ate garri at that time.'

 (b)   mì ndílì áʔ garri púndɛ nì
       I eat Neg garri time that
       'I did not eat garri at that time.'

5.4.1.2.4 *The Future Tense*
The future tense in Nfaw is marked by a rising tone on the subject marker. The negative particle for this tense is ʃɛ̌ (same as for the present). The third person plural however behaves peculiarly, taking its tonal tense morpheme on the verb rather than the subject marker. It equally has a separate negative particle *sî*, such as in (67).

(67a) hanna á kwə̀ bwê
      Hannah SM cut trees
      'Hannah will cut down the trees.'

 (b) hanna á ʃɛ̌ kwə̀ bwê
      Hannah SM Neg cut trees
      'Hannah will not cut down trees.'

(68a) bá dʒǐ nkwì
      they cry night
      'They will cry at night.'

 (b) bá sî dʒì nkwì
      they Neg cry night
      'They will not cry at night.'

Note that in this tense the use of *áwə* or *áʔ* is unacceptable as illustrated by the ungrammaticality of (69)

(69)* bá áwə dʒì nkwì
they Neg cry night
'They will not cry at night.'

It is worth noting that the negative marker could be elided on the introduction of the aspectual marker ə. In such cases, the aspectual marker bears a rising tone as shown in (70) below.

(70a) bá bí nàn mámwòn
they be chase birds
'They chased away the birds.'

(b) bá bí áʔ ə nàn mámwòn
they be Neg Asp chase birds
'They did not chase away the birds.'

(c) bá bí ə̌ nàn mámwòn
they be Asp chase birds
'They did not chase away the birds.'

In this section, the link between negative markers and tense has been discussed. It has been established that the choice of negative particle is greatly influenced by tense. ʃɛ̌ applies to actions in the present and future tenses while áwə and áʔ apply to the past tense.

5.4.2 Negation and Sentence Structure

The form of the negative particle in Nfaw may also depend on the sentence type. In this section we examine the nature of negation in various sentence types.

5.4.2.1 Negation in Imperative Sentences.

Imperative sentences as mentioned earlier present commands or directions. Such sentences are characteristically short, often consisting of the verb only, or the verb and its complement. Imperative sentences are negated in Nfaw by the morpheme òsì ('not'), as in (71).

(71a) jǎn   'Buy!'
     kə̀   ' Go!'
     búngú   'Run!'

(b) òsì ján   'Don't buy!'
    òsì kə́   'Don't go!'
    òsì búngú   'Don't run!'

When the negation of a constituent is intended to serve the semantic function of discontinuing an action which was initiated, or refuting a previously stated proposition, the postverbal morpheme *pə* "any longer" is introduced, as in (72).

(72a) jǎn radio   'Buy a radio!'
(b) òsì ján pə radio 'Don't buy a radio any longer!'

The examples above show that the rising tone on verbs like *jǎn* simplifies to a high in the negative. This is probably for emphasis, as a high pitch is emphatic.

5.4.2.2 Negation in Relative Clauses.

The relative clause in Nfaw is introduced by two markers: *jə* and *àwə* Relative clauses are negated by the morphemes *sǎ* and *áʔ*. Thus for sentences with a relative clause, there are two possibilities of negation:

      (i) Where the scope of the negative particle is the relative clause, (in which case *sǎ* is used); and

      (ii) Where the entire proposition is rendered negative, (where *áʔ* is used)

Consider the following sentences:
(73a) mɔʔ àwə à   dí fá   à   wílí
      man Rel SM is here SM died
'The man who was here is dead.'

(b) mɔ̀ʔ àwə ǐ sǎ fá à wílí
    man Rel SM Neg here SM died
    'The man who is not here is dead.'

(c) mɔ̀ʔ àwə à dí fá à wílí áʔ
    man Rel SM is here SM dead Neg
    'The man who is here is not dead.'

In (73b), the subject marker changes from à to ǐ. We assume that this still functions as SM because of its syntactic position. This change is accompanied by the omission of the verb "be". Following our earlier postulation, this is certainly another manifestation of the cliticization of the copula in this language. It is obvious that while (73c) negates the proposition (the man is not dead), (73b) negates only the relative clause (the man who is not here). The interesting observation here is that Nfaw uses separate negative particles for each.

5.4.2.3 Clauses Stating Purpose

Such clauses state purpose of a situation contained in a matrix clause. The linking phrase *líbwènà,* ("so that", "in order that", etc) introduces such clauses in Nfaw. Clauses stating purpose are negated by the morpheme sì , as in (74) and (75).

(74a) mbone à ké á wə á líbwènà ekoko à kwî
      Mbone SM go Prep there in order   Ekoko SM annoy
      'Mbone has gone there in order to make Ekoko angry.'

(b) mbone à ké á wə á líbwènà ekoko sì kwî
    Mbone SM go Prep there in order   Ekoko Neg annoy
    'Mbone has gone there in order not to annoy Ekoko.'

(75a) pǎ à líbwènà mì kwì
      come so that   I   annoy
      'Come so that I may be angry.'

(b) pă   à   líbwὲnà   mì   sì   kwì
    come so   that   me   Neg   annoy
    'Come so that I may not be angry.'

5.4.2.4 Constituent Negation and Contrastive Emphasis

The particle *sà káká* ("it is not") is employed in the negation of constituent structures like the NP. This particle precedes the constituent, as in (76) and (77).

(76) sà káká john   'It is not John.'

(77) sà káká bìyì   'It is not yams.'

The negation of constituents as in (76) above, has the semantic implication of contrastive emphasis. In addition to denying the fact that it is John, (76) suggests that it is someone else.

5.4.2.5 Constituent Negation and the Focus Marker

The focus marker serves to focalize constituents in a sentence. The use of both the focus marker and constituent negation as in (77), brings about contrastive focus.

(77a) sà káká bìyì bó mi nɨɲíní
      it Neg yams Foc I like
      ' It is not yams I like.'

(b) sà káká nó à kə́ á ŋkí
    it Neg Foc SM go Prep home
    'It was not him who went home.'

(77a) above is to be interpreted as meaning that the speaker does not like yams but likes something else. In Nfaw, it is possible to use more than one focus marker in a construction. The resultant construction gets an emphatic interpretation. When used in this way, it also has the semantic effect of contrastive focus as in (78).

(78a) sarah mɔ́ miɔ   mɔ́   à mínі́ jɔ
    Sarah Foc herself Foc SM look it
    'Sarah looked for it (herself).'

The examples in (77) and (78) also show slight differences in the form of the focus marker, specifically in terms of the initial consonant. Given that Nfaw is a noun class language; these differences can readily be attributed to the difference in noun class of the focused constituents. In fact, in most noun class languages, particles tend to take the class prefix of the noun they modify.

When more than one focus marker is used in a sentence the negative marker is *séna* as exemplified in (78b).

(78b) se séna sarah mɔ́   miɔ   mɔ́ à   mínі́ jɔ
    it Neg Sarah Foc herself Foc   SM   look   it
    'It is not Sarah herself who looked for it.'

Semantically, the denial in (78a) above is not of the proposition (X looked for it), but the focus of attention that Sarah herself "looked for it". The tacit implication of this denial is that someone else looked for it. A similar situation obtains in (79) where only the focus is denied.

(79a) bəɲǎ   bǎn   bɔ́   bé búngú bǎn   mùlkɔ?
    Mothers children Foc   SM take   children care
    'It is only mothers who take care of children'

(b) sà ká bəɲǎ   bǎn bɔ́ bé búngu bǎn mùlkɔ?
    it Neg mothers children Foc SM   take children care
    'It is not only mothers that take care of children'

In (79b) *ká* (which is the shortened form of *káká*) is employed. The full form, *káká*, is certainly a reduplication of this morpheme and both are used as free variants.

5.4.2.6 Double Negatives in Nfaw

We refer here to the use of more than one negative particle in a construction. In complex sentences like (80), the use of more than one negative particle can be explained on semantic grounds.

(80) mɔʔ àwə sǎ fa à wílì áʔ
    man who Neg here SM die Neg
    'The man who is not here is not dead.'

In this construction, the first negative morpheme sǎ negates the embedded relative clause while the second áʔ negates the matrix clause. One also notices that it is possible to omit the subject marker when the copula is omitted as in (80) above. On the contrary this is not the case in situations where the verb is not omitted as in (73c). The resultant semantic implication is given in (81) and (82).

(81) the man who is not here.

(82) the man is not dead.

Example (80) in effect subsumes the negative constructions in (71) and (72). However, in simple sentences like (83), there is no semantic motivation for using more than one negative particle.

(83) sɛ́ ʃî pílì áʔ
    we Neg come Neg
    'We have not come.'

(84) mi ʃî kwɔ̀ŋ áʔ
    I Neg sing Neg
    'I will not sing.'

The kind of double negation in (83) and (84) is for very emphatic pragmatic situations. (83) and (84) therefore exemplify double negation while (80) is only apparently an example of double negation. Double negation is rarely elicited from Nfaw speakers as translation for negative sentences. It is however a possibility and speakers employ such utterances depending on the amount of emphasis they seek to convey. When transitive verbs are used, the negative morpheme *áʔ* is positioned before the complement of the verb as in (85) and (86). This shows that the position of the negative particle is immediate post verbal and not absolute sentence final.

(85) bá sî kwɔ̀ŋ áʔ mìkonè
    they Neg sing Neg song
    'They will not sing a song.'

(86) mì ndílì áʔ garri púndɛ nì
    I eat Neg garri time that

'I did not eat garri at that time.'

In this section, we have described the various negative morphemes in Nfaw and their contexts of use. Apart from *áwə* and *áʔ*, which are used as free variants, the other morphemes have been found to be tagged to tenses and sentence types. This distribution is summarized below.

Negative Marker	Context Of Use
ʃɛ̆	Present / future tense
áwə	P1
áʔ	P1, P2, P3
sî	Future (3rd person)
òsì	Imperative
sǎ	Relative clause
sì	Purpose clause
káká / ká	Constituent
séna	Focused construction

5.5 Conclusion

We set out in this chapter to overview the syntactic structure of Nfaw. Some of the negative morphemes in this language *(áwǝ* and *áʔ)* have been found to be used in free variation while the rest are determined by tense or sentence type. The distribution of negation morphemes is intriguing in the sense that while some of the morphemes occur in preverbal position, others occur postverbally. Finally, it is possible in this language to use double negatives depending on the amount of emphasis the speaker seeks to convey.

---

1. The following abbreviations have been used throughout this paper: Foc = Focus word, HL = Falling tone, LH = Rising tone, Neg = Negation, P1 = Immediate past, P2 = Non-too-distant past, P3 = Remote past, SM = Subject marker, Loc =Locative particle, Asp = Aspectual marker, Rel = Relative pronoun, Prep = Preposition, Prog = progressive

2. It is not clear what this morpheme stands for but it is likely to be a verbal extension.

References

Chumbow, Sammy & Pius Tamanji 1994 "Bafut", In Peter Kahrel & René Van Den Berg (eds), *Typological Studies in Negation*, John Benjamins, Amsterdam.

Grimes, Barbara 2000 *Ethnologue: Languages of the World*, SIL, Texas.

Lyonga, Ngoisah 2002 "The Morphology of the Noun Phrase and the Verb Phrase in Mokpe in Relation to Orthography", M.A Thesis, University of Buea.

Mutaka, Ngessimo 2000 *Introduction to African Linguistics (with the collaboration of Pius Ngwa Tamanji)*, Munich: Lincom Europa.

Mendandi, Abbo 2003 "Negation in Tupuri", B.A project, University of Buea.

Mensah, Eyo 2001 "Negation in Efik", Kiabara Journal of Humanities, pp 61-67.

Tanda, Vincent & Ayu'nwi Neba 2006 "Negation in Mokpe and Two Related Coastal Bantu Languages of Cameroon" *African Study Monographs*, pp 201-219.

Trask, Robert 1993 *A Dictionary of Grammatical Terms in Linguistics*, London and New York, Routledge.

Chapter Six
Towards the Development of a Functional Bafaw Literacy Programme

Blasius Agha-ah Chiatoh

6.0 Introduction

One of the primary factors that militate in favour of language endangerment in extreme multilingual settings such as Cameroon is their minority status. This process is compounded by language contact and the accompanying shift in language attitude of native speakers of minority languages brought about by the presence of prestige languages (usually foreign languages) in education. Whether or not literacy programmes succeed in these languages is, therefore, to be measured from the degree to which communities value their languages and want to see them promoted as instruments of learning.

In the light of the above, therefore, it is vitally important that the community not only understand but also recognise that the survival of its language and its ability to effectively contribute to change processes depend on the degree to which it serves as a medium of instruction at least at the basic level. In Africa where illiteracy rates are still alarmingly high, the promotion of adult literacy programmes in national languages constitutes a major link not only in reducing illiteracy but also in overall community development planning. Here lies the relevance of community literacy programmes. It is closely linked to the question of language choice in formal and non-formal learning.

However, such literacy initiative should not be limited to the language question but systematically integrated into the values, resources and efforts of the members of the community. This means that the community must recognise literacy as a joint enterprise that requires collective human and material input. In fact, it should be perceived as a venture in which progress is guaranteed by all (ordinary people, trained personnel and established leadership). Collective and individual motivation as well as a high level of volunteerism is indispensable in initiating and sustaining the literacy enterprise.

In this presentation, I examine the possibilities for establishing a literacy programme for the Bafaw people within the framework of the dynamics of planned social change or what is commonly referred to as community development.

6.1. Language, literacy and planned change

All change processes take place in a language of some kind. Literacy, which is not only the ability to read and write but also a process of empowerment for individual and collective change, takes place fundamentally in the languages of the learners. In setting up a literacy programme for a community, there is need to consider the language of instruction and the overall social impact the programme is likely to have on the community. The attitudes of native speakers towards their language also constitute a major area of interest for literacy planners and implementers. And more often than not, these attitudes have to do with their perception of the value of their language.

In initiating literacy programmes, therefore, promoters should seek to address the crucial issues that affect community attitudes. These issues have been raised and argued by many a linguist across the world. We need, therefore, not tarry on this here. However, one thing needs to be clarified. It is the fact that ideally, literacy takes place in the first language (mother tongue) of the learners and in Africa these are almost always indigenous languages (Obanya, 2000). When initial reading and writing is conducted in a language other than the mother tongue, this is, in fact, no longer literacy but a process in second, third, etc. language learning. The issue here is that we cannot talk of second or third language learning in the absence of the first. In other words, basic literacy is only literacy when it has its starting point in the first language. Non-respect for this principle will have serious negative effects on the cognitive and creative development processes of the learners even if they end up functioning in the non-first language in question. When this happens, the entire learning process is stunted and consequently, cannot constitute solid enough grounds for meaningful individual and social change. These negative effects are to be observed in the manner in which the new-literate perceives the world and interacts in it.

As early as 1953, UNESCO recognised the language problem in literacy when it recommended the use of mother tongues in basic learning, recommendations that have become today, a global reference orientation to countries that desire to make real major strides in literacy promotion business. In these recommendations, it specifies three levels of utility of mother tongues not only in education but also in the entire development process of communities. These are the psychological, sociological and educational levels as revealed in the observation below:

> Psychologically, it is the system of meaningful signs that in his mind works automatically for expression and understanding. Sociologically, it is the means of identification among the members of the community to which he belongs. Educationally, he learns more quickly through it than through an unfamiliar linguistic medium.

As can be observed, the benefits to be reaped from planning basic education founded on mother tongues are enormous and varied. As such, any attempt to exclude mother tongues in educational planning would consequently not facilitate meaningful planned change in the society. Learning practices with foreign languages as their basis, as is the case in Cameroon, should not constitute the ideal but rather the exception. And indeed, there is no justification for such an exception.

Planned change in linguistically heterogeneous communities thus involves careful language options. In choosing the language of learning, planners are indirectly involved in orienting and shaping change processes in the society. In the case of minority versus majority languages, the choice of the former and the accommodation of the latter in literacy and formal mother tongue education programmes will certainly yield the best possible dividends (Heugh, 2000: 7). It is on these grounds that I examine the difficulties encountered and then the requirements for establishing a functional literacy programme for the Bafaw community.

6.2 Literacy as a community initiative

One of the major ideas the National Association of Cameroonian Language Committees (NACALCO) and its Centre for Applied Linguistics has developed within the past decade the concept of local ownership (Tadadjeu, Mba & Chiatoh, 2001:2-30), a concept that has been further refined to mean community response (Chiatoh, 2004). Underlying these two concepts is the necessity to arouse, within the community of native speakers of the language being promoted, local interest and pride, and subsequently local support, the basis for self-sustaining promotion of learning in national languages. It is based on the fact that absence of local input at both material and human resource levels breeds near-total dependence on external sources for the promotion of literacy.

In fact, nearly all the programmes in Cameroon are set up by expatriates either operating within the framework of the Summer Institute of Linguistics (SIL) or the church particularly the Lutheran Evangelical Church of Cameroon and the Catholic Church. NACALCO, a national non-governmental body, and the umbrella organisation within which local language committees operate, only comes into the process after the language committee would have been established. At its creation in 1989, it was primarily concerned with coordinating and supervising the literacy activities of its members. It is only recently that it became involved standardisation initiatives with the implementation of the Basic Standardisation of All African Languages (BASAL) project. Through BASAL, volunteer linguists are assigned to communities and after putting in place an alphabet, a writing system, basic didactic materials and trained local personnel, they also help in setting up language committees to pursue activities they have started. But like others, these committees have not developed autonomous capacities for ensuring continuity.

Coming back to experts, they possess the resources to cater for various aspects of the programme. The problem which arises is that eventually, when they withdraw, they do so with all these resources, thus leaving behind a vacuum that the community is not prepared to fill. They cannot support and sustain activities and so the programme loses steam and sometimes, even phases out entirely. Cases observed in some communities give reason to worry about the future of programmes set up by external bodies and individuals. The Babungo,

Tikar and Vute examples (Nforbi, 2003:47-61) are a reflection of this. Nforbi reports that after the completion of the Babungo Bible translation work, activities regressed remarkably with copies of the Bible piled up at one corner of the translator's premises without even the Church for which it was translated taking over the project. Concerning the Tikar, in the literacy office in Bankim, large stocks of Christian literature and primers are packed among other things particularly food on the shelves and with the Vute, the language committee exists simply in name. Literacy activities are considered as a church affair and even the chairperson of the committee cannot control them.

This grim picture points to the fact that an ideal literacy initiative is one that emanates from within the community or at worst, that which is triggered by an external force but systematically built into a community-based enterprise. This is almost what happened with the Bafaw community. An initiative that developed from the community failed to generate the necessary local support.

6.3 The language committee as the nerve centre of community literacy

A striking characteristic of literacy is that, unlike formal education, it is a delicate undertaking. It does not only deal with adults, who have different perceptions, long-established attitudes and concerns, but it also involves employing different methods, strategies and techniques of promoting learning in the community. As such, it becomes necessary to always adapt literacy objectives and programme implementation strategies to specific contextual realities. In Cameroon, it has been revealed that successful literacy planning and management is extremely difficult, if not impossible, if this does not take place through a functional and dynamic language committee (LC).

A language committee is a local non-governmental agency established by the community to cater for the enterprise of language development and promotion. It is a cultural organisation responsible for promoting the cultural values of the community through formal education and literacy in its language. In this respect, the LC oversees the planning, implementation and evaluation of activities. Its appellation varies from one community to another but its functions remain fundamentally the same. In some areas it is referred to as organisation and in others as association. The essential thing though is that it actually plays the role of an academy, spearheading language standardisation, modernisation and quality promotion in all domains of written communication. In their discussion of the Cameroonian experience in adult literacy, Sadembouo et al (1999:277) underscore the leading role of the LC in the following:

> A language committee can be looked at as the managing body responsible for conception and execution, initiation and guiding of the production and popularization of the use of written literature, and organizing the training of necessary personnel for adult literacy and education.

In addition to the above scientific tasks the language committee also undertakes other kinds of activities such as sensitisation and mobilisation of resources. However, it must be retained that the mere existence of a committee in the community does not guarantee effective promotion of learning. How properly it functions depends on other factors such as the choice of members, structural organisation, available resources, community perception and support and the cultural framework within which it functions. In some areas, the LC is integrated into Cultural and Development Organisations. In the Meta community for instance, the promotion of the language is inscribed in the constitution of the Meta Cultural and Development Association (MECUDA). The latter are elite structures committed to piloting self-reliant development through the mobilisation of resources for various community projects. As a cultural organisation, it is desirable that the LC function within an established elite cultural group. But it must watch against too much reliance on politicians who can transform purely development initiatives into political propaganda. So, if the principles on and objectives for which the committee is established are not well-thought out, it may remain just a rubber stamp. Mbguagbaw (2000: 414) confirms this view when he notes:

> Some language committees are just there by name. Very little comes from them. They rely mostly on the SIL/literacy consultants. In some cases, they

have no document on how they operate. It is advisable that a language committee function within a development association in its language area. This will provide an infrastructure for it to work under. This will help in bringing in elite who work outside of the community to develop interest in their language.

An ideal language committee is one that is representative of the entire community of native speakers of the language through the integration of members of all the varieties of the language and the different classes of people in the community. But above all, it consists of people who are highly motivated and available to undertake the promotion of activities. These are people whose fundamental pleasure is to sow the seeds of development and to see these bear fruits, indeed, really good fruits. It is this spirit that renders the committee dynamic and functional.

This spirit aside, the committee must be well structured, that is, it should clearly differentiate between the different functions of the various governing organs. For instance, a clear distinction should be made between administrative, scientific and technical responsibilities. Also, as an academy, it is vital that the committee controls all language development activities in the community. Even if activities such as Bible translation are coordinated and monitored by a different agency, it is advisable that these be integrated into the general framework of the committee. Mbuagbaw (2000:414 ibid) prescribes a supervisory role for the LC in all language activities in the following words:

> If the impetus for beginning a language committee is to produce literacy materials and translate the Bible, it is important to form two sub-committees - one for the general literacy and the other for Bible translation, both functioning under the umbrella of the language committee.

The quality of committee members too matters. Apart from being motivated and available, the ideal is for them to be literate in their language so as to be able to motivate others to learn and promote learning. This ensures that reading and writing become core values and characteristics of the committee and of the entire community. What all these views represent is that special care should be taken in setting up and running a language committee. Sadembouo (1996:5) proposes crucial steps for establishing a language committee. Because of their determining role in building LC continuity, functioning and dynamism, I produce them here integrally.

1. Start with one individual who wants to develop the language, someone highly motivated.
2. This person needs to meet an influential community member to share his/her vision for the development of the language.
3. The two need to prioritise which domains of language they want to begin promoting. They should seek to choose things that the general populace loves, something that would be highly desired to have in print. This could be scriptures, songs, stories, an agenda or diary, etc.
4. Send a qualified person to learn about language development (SIL courses for instance). This training, of course, would begin with orthography development and progress from there.
5. Develop the language committee nucleus by: a) Choosing men and women from leaders of the community b) Choosing representatives from the various villages (cities) of the various dialects. c) Go ahead and start the work for a period of time (until stage 6 is a reality). With a standardised orthography in hand, choose which work to publish. This could be any of the following; songs, hymns, agendas for the next year, Christmas story, folk story, etc.
6. Call a general assembly to start the formal language committee: a) Invite authorities of the village, elites from the whole country, village people, in essence, people from all walks of life. b) Goals for this general assembly include: setting up statutes (constitution of the language committee), plan next year's literacy or/and language development programme, election of officers, establishing an office

(physical structure or/and personnel), and financial considerations.

As can be observed, a lot of caution needs to be exercised in setting up a language committee. When the LC has been fully established, it would be necessary to go further and legalise it and empower it with an autonomous site. While legalisation gives legality to the LC, an autonomous site offers it an imposing personality. Both elements give the LC recognition and credibility, facilitating the execution of action plans.

6.4 The Bafaws in the dynamics of social change

According to Grimes (1996:190), the Bafaw community has a population of 8,400 people. But Chia (2006), in "A sociolinguistic survey of the Bafaw language" (in this volume), thinks that these figures should be much less. According to him, Grimes' estimates actually represent the population of two communities, Bafaw and Balong and that the latter has a far larger population. This means that the language is endangered not only because of its extreme minority status but also because there is lack of an educational system to encourage and support its written use. In addition to this number, one can count many other thousands of people from other parts of Cameroon and beyond. This makes the community one of the most heterogeneous and dynamic communities in this region of the country. And who talks about heterogeneity, talks about diversity in languages, ideas and values, in short, in socio-cultural dynamics.

In this kind of community, there is bound to be one or the other of two effects. Either heterogeneity enhances the process of planned social change or it impedes it. Heterogeneity facilitates social change when the diverse resources of the community are carefully harnessed for the betterment of the community. On the other hand, it impedes change when these same resources, because not easily coordinated, are dispersed. Among these resources, language and culture are perhaps the most crucial. And talking about language, it should be recalled that contact between languages brings about gradual but steady shifts in linguistic attitudes of native speakers of minority languages. Generally, the impact is not very desirable. Minority language users tend to develop admiration for prestige languages because of their presence in controlling domains such as administration and education.

Planned social change requires above everything else, the presence of an adequate educational system for the promotion of values upheld by the society. Such a system should address learning as a holistic, permanent and continuing enterprise first by way of its language in education options and through structural planning and organisation. By holistic, I mean that the system should consider formal education and adult literacy as part and parcel of the same whole and to recognise that the absence of one directly affects the functioning of the other. Experience shows that in highly heterogeneous communities such as Bafaw, important phenomena such as volunteerism, social cohesion and external elite support are crucial in the success of social change processes. These are key ingredients in building an enabling atmosphere for culture-based change processes. They are central in the establishment and smooth running of literacy and educational programmes.

6.5 Attempts at setting up a Bafaw literacy programme

One of the priority requirements for successful community literacy is the presence of local specialists. These are people trained in various aspects of language development and promotion. In the 90s, some two natives, John Akwo and Peter Dibo (graduates of the Higher Teachers' Training College – ENS Yaounde) received training in the SIL-organised Discover Your Language Course (DYL) in Yaounde. This course, today referred to as First Steps, equips people interested in promoting their languages with basic linguistic tools such as phonological analysis, semantics, grammar and orthography development. As the nucleus of language promotion activities, the two men set themselves to elaborating the first Lifɔ primer draft between 1997 and 1998. The primer was examined and confirmed for printing by the NACALCO Centre for Applied Linguistics (CLA) which showed a lot of interest in assisting the community to set up a literacy programme.

To encourage the initiatives, NACALCO supported them in organising a training seminar for literacy trainers and mother tongue education teachers. They were also given the opportunity to host a centre for the Southwest region. This centre would accommodate communities more experienced in literacy (Akoose, Kenyang, Ejagham and Denya) until each of the communities would deem it necessity to own its separate centre. In normal situations, the centre would have gone to another area. This is not to say though that this constituted the only reason for creating the centre. Other reasons that underlay the granting of this venue were accessibility to the other communities, motivation to receive other communities and then actual preparedness to host a centre. And the Bafaws, although new in literacy matters, were not only centrally located but also expressed the willingness to host the centre. Eventually, other languages of the region like Bakweri and Oroko would join this group of languages. The centre was then granted and hosted by the Government Teachers' Training College Kumba thanks to the collaboration of one of the local specialists, Mr John Akwo (then Vice-Principal) of the school.

In September 1998, the two Lifɔ technicians successfully planned and organised the first ever training seminar within the framework Operational Research Programme for Language Education in Cameroon (Propelca), one of NACALCO's main programmes. Together with a colleague, Dr Gratiana Ndamsah, we conducted this seminar which traditionally runs for two weeks. The course brought together five languages of the South West Province – Lifɔ, Kenyang, Denya, Ejagham and Akoose. A total of 33 participants attended the course with a third of them coming from the Bafaw community. While the goal for the Bafaw community was to set up adult literacy and mother tongue education activities, that for the other communities was principally to introduce formal mother tongue use in schools since they were already involved in adult literacy and even informal mother tongue classes. Bafaw participants exhibited a high level of motivation and enthusiasm.

If the Bafaws succeeded in establishing a programme, based essentially on local impetus, this would constitute a case study for literacy specialists and planners. Regrettably, the contrary happened and close to a decade afterwards, what seemed a very promising opportunity, no longer has any traces of relevance in the community. The initiative died down as soon as the training was over. No single adult literacy or mother tongue education class ever went operational and neither community leadership nor the local technicians, seemed to realise that a valuable opportunity had been lost.

6.6 Could the Bafaw initiative have succeeded?

A look at the initiatives, that is, the training received by the local specialists, the elaboration of the primer and the organisation of the training seminar, indicate that there was some significant local enthusiasm, at least on the part of the local technicians, to set up a literacy programme. But good intensions, if not well put into practice, can yield negative results. It seems that the good intensions of the local technicians were not well nurtured and that some crucial phases of the planning process were either neglected or completely ignored. These can be summed up as the lack of initial preparation and absence of community leadership involvement.

6.6.1. Initial preparation of the community

Initial preparation of the community accounts significantly for its success or failure in literacy organisation. Prior to and during the implementation process, the community needs to be adequately sensitised and educated on the importance of promoting literacy in its language. This is especially relevant in Africa where literacy in local languages has been relegated to the background for many decades. People need to understand and be convinced that their needs and aspirations in all their dimensions (social, cultural, economic and political) are fully integrated into the programme. The future life of the programme depends on the success or failure registered at this level.

From the look of things, this phase of the Bafaw initiative was either largely ignored or insufficiently stressed as activities started and ended with the two local technicians. As such, the two technicians did not receive enough local support. For instance, NACALCO's attempts to fund the printing of the primer ended in a fiasco because the authors were disappointed by the community leadership's inability to make financial compensation for the elaboration work. It is worthy to note here that NACALCO funding for material production takes place in the form of subsidies and so is never directed at any individual but rather at the entire community through the language committee. Proceeds from sales of such materials do not go to the author(s) but are reinvested into the committee in the form of revolving funds, a concept developed to help facilitate the building of committee financial autonomy. This did not seem to be any attractive solution to the authors' compensation problem.

6.6.2. Absence of community leadership involvement
If literacy promotion is essentially a collective community affair, then even if a few people act, as happens within the framework of the language committee, this should be done on behalf of the entire community. Engaging key members of the community in decision-making at the conception, planning and implementation phases and considering their opinions is an essential ingredient of smooth programme management in traditional Cameroonian communities. In these communities, traditional rulers are respected as a matter of course so much so that development initiatives that do not receive their approval and benediction are most likely not to enjoy community-wide acceptance and support.

The two Lifɔ technicians, either by intention or omission, failed to de-concentrate their powers and so became the sole figures around the entire programme. Again, they could not devote sufficient time to activities given that they were civil servants. In fact, the hope was that the 1998 training would produce some local persons who were a little freer to pilot activities. This is actually what obtains with the rest of the programmes around the country. In these other communities, permanent personnel are mostly retired workers (preferably schoolteachers) and young people trained in literacy management.

It seems thus that even if any other factors did account for the inability of the Bafaw literacy initiative to take off the ground, the central issue lay in the lack of community preparation and rather too much concentration of power around two people who were not free enough to ensure permanent supervision of activities.

6.7 Considerations for establishing a functional Bafaw literacy programme

Programme continuity is not an accidental occurrence; it is the result of thoughtful conception and strategising in line with implementation approaches and methods. And so whether motivation for the initiative emanates from the community or from without, caution is indispensable. When motivation comes from within, care should be taken to avoid personalisation of the programme. And where the programme is externally motivated, there is also need to guard against the spirit of dependence.

To guard against any such eventuality, literacy goals and objectives as well as implementation strategies must be carefully tailored to match contextual realities. In addition, the initiative needs to be built into a shared community vision so that activities are not simply regarded as a programme but rather as a new way of perceiving reality, indeed, a new set of values. Effective planning for continuity could be guaranteed if the following factors are taken into account from the very onset:

6.7.1 A functional and dynamic language committee

As we have indicated above, a language committee constitutes the cornerstone of any literacy endeavour in our context. This committee should function on a daily basis and be capable of providing the materials and services that the community needs to undertake learning in its language. A dynamic and functional committee is one that possesses not only skilled personnel but also enjoys maximum community support, a strong public image and is capable of mobilising resources for self-sustenance. Functionality and dynamism are closely linked to the choice of personnel, community synergy and support, public appreciation and financial independence.

And above everything else, financial independence seems to occupy front stage because with self-supporting finances, all other problems encountered in the language promotion enterprise can easily be resolved. With autonomous resources, the committee is capable of building a strong institutional personality necessary for the survival of the programme.

6.7.2 Collective local ownership

Community literacy is a collective enterprise, that is, the affair of the entire community even if this is spearheaded by a given individual or group of individuals. For activities to run smoothly and consequently take root, the community must take ownership of the scientific and material resource aspects of the programme. This necessitates that the community first accepts, participates in and then undertakes to sustain the programme over time (Chiatoh, 2004). This means that the LC needs to gain the support of the community especially the local and external elite. These people are needed for raising autonomous funds without which the LC remains financially fragile and incapacitated. The ability to mobilise funds gives the LC some degree of independence, credibility and security.

But ownership in itself is an extremely challenging objective to attain for this actually implies self-sustenance. Strong local synergy, built around language development particularly with respect to income generation, is, therefore, indispensable. This synergy is nurtured, maintained and continually strengthened through the language committee together with established institutions such as traditional authorities, local councils and elite groups. However, care must be taken to avoid unnecessary reliance on political elite who can easily transform language issues into political propaganda.

6.7.3 An enabling environment

An environment is enabling when it encourages the growth of reading and writing practices in the language. The ultimate goal of a literacy programme is to transform the community from one constructed on oral tradition to one that functions on the basis of both oral and written communication. A literate or an enabling environment is, therefore, one in which there are maximum resources and motivation for reading and writing practices to flourish in the language. This includes the willingness and ability of community members to produce and use literature.

Building a literate environment implies empowering the community to produce and use didactic materials as well as diversified literature in its language. The importance of an enabling environment in community literacy success is captured by UNESCO (2005:207) when it notes:

> In neighbourhoods and communities, a rich literate environment would have numerous signs, posters and handbills, as well as literacy-promoting institutions such as schools, offices, courts, libraries, banks and training centres. And yet, literate environments are more than places offering access to printed matter, written records, visual materials and advanced technologies; ideally, they should enable the free

exchange of information and provide an array of opportunities for lifelong learning.

In the initial stages of the programme, this literature may be limited to didactic materials but gradually, this must evolve to include brochures, signboards, novels, theatre, etc and any other form of written materials that enhance, consolidate and sustain the reading and writing process. Creating such an environment also calls for the establishment of an efficient distribution system that enables the literature produced to be available to the whole community. In short, it makes sure that those who desire to read find sufficient literature meet their desires.

6.7.4 A high spirit of volunteerism among workers
A high level of volunteerism among members of the language committee is essential in the successful implementation of activities. In Cameroon, where indigenous languages cannot yet generate financial benefits, deep sentimental motivation is indispensable. Government does not promote national language activities and language committees are not yet capable of generating the required financial resources for the remuneration of personnel. Steady growth in the number of language committees in the country is not accompanied by a corresponding growth in resources for the language development endeavour (Chiatoh, 2001:6). Those who work in the programme, therefore, should be motivated enough to offer their time, services and even resources to ensure the success of activities.

But volunteerism could also become counter productive if over-stretched, that is, if it tends to last for too long. Initially, therefore, the solution lies in what the community wants and on the choice of workers. The essential thing, though, is for committee management to realise that volunteerism is a transitional quality and that with ever rising socio-economic pressures, volunteer positions should progressively be transformed into permanent career positions (Chiatoh, 2002 ibid).

6.7.5. Adult literacy and formal mother tongue education

A successful literacy programme is one that has set up effective classes in the language of the community, in other words, an ongoing educational system. But for an education system to be productive, it needs to create a logical complementary link between the school and the community as inseparable stakeholders in the learning process. So, a system that promotes adult literacy in the absence of formal mother tongue education or vice-versa is incomplete and so cannot deliver the desired goods. Both the community and the school environments should contribute to the promotion and sustenance of learning. In doing so, they benefit mutually from their experiences, thereby, rendering learning more effective and impacting. This is especially relevant in the domain of mother tongue promotion as a majority of the children stem from homes where the only medium of daily communication is an indigenous language. In this type of situation, learning stops as soon as children leave the school milieu. In the same manner, parents' knowledge cannot be exploited to the benefit of the children and vice-versa.

Community adult literacy classes, therefore, should aim among other things, to trigger, encourage and oversee the introduction of the language into the school system. Our Cameroonian experience reveals that formal mother tongue education is especially successful in communities that run functional adult literacy classes. The complementary promotion of these components of the programme helps in bridging the gap between the world of the home and that of the school, thereby, guaranteeing programme rooting and wide-ranging impact.

6.8 Conclusion

I have established the relevance of mother tongue adult literacy in the process of social change in minority language settings in general and within the framework of planning, reviving and managing literacy in the Bafaw community in particular. In doing so, I have highlighted the historical background of the Lifɔ language development initiative and suggested steps for setting up a functional and dynamic literacy programme. The leading role of a language committee as the cornerstone of every literacy initiative in Cameroon has also been brought out. The issues raised here should, given the chance, lead to the revival and sustenance of the Bafaw literacy programme.

References

Chia, E.N. 2006 "The Bafaw Language: A Sociolinguistic Survey" Unpublished Paper, University of Buea.

Chiatoh, A.B. 2001 "Towards a Model for Predicting an Autonomous Literacy Threshold in Cameroon" AJAL N° 02, CLA

Chiatoh, A.B. 2002 "The Career Supervisor and Mother Tongue Education Generalisation in Cameroon" AJAL N° 03, CLA

Chiatoh, A.B. 2004 Assessing Community Response to Mother Tongue Literacy in Multilingual Context: The Case of Cameroon. PhD Thesis University of Yaounde 1

Heugh, K. 2000 A case against Mother Tongue-based Bilingual Education in South Africa. PRAESA Occasional Papers N° 6 University of Cape Town

Mbuagbaw, C.T. 2000 "Language Engineering in Cameroon" In Lébikaza, K.K. (ed) Actes du 3è Congrès Mondial de Linguistique Africaine. Rudigger Koppe Verlag Koln

Nforbi, E. 2003 "Community involvement in Mother-tongue education through a dynamic functional language committee" AJAL N° 04, CLA

Obanya, P. 2000 "Learning In, With, and From the First Language" PRAESA Occasional Papers N° 19 University of Cape Town

Sadembouo, E. 1996 "Starting a Language Committee" (Lecture notes) In An Introduction to Literacy Principles, Methods and Materials. , Yaounde, SIL.

Sadembouo, E et al. 1999 "Cameroonian Experience in the Organization of Adult Education" In Organizing and Structuring Adult Education UNESCO, Paris, Osaka University, Japan

Tadadjeu, M, Mba, G & Chiatoh, A.B. 2001 "The Process of Local Ownership of Multilingual Education in Cameroon" AJAL N° 02, CLA

UNESCO 1953 The Use of Vernacular Languages in Education Monographs on Fundamental Education N° 08. Paris, UNESCO.

UNESCO 2005 Literacy For Life: EFA Global Monitoring Report. Paris

Chapter Seven

A Review of Nfaw Orthography: Some Proposals

Ayu'nwi N. Neba

7.0 Introduction

Having considered sociolinguistic situation of Nfaw, aspects of the sound system, the morphology, syntax and literacy, it is relevant to pause a little on the orthography of this language.

As a matter of fact, during our research, we discovered that there was already some form of an alphabet for the language. Some youths were already trained on how to write using the alphabet. In this section we present the existing writing system with some adjustments based on the general principles proposed in the General Alphabet of Cameroon Languages (Tadadjeu and Sademnbouo (1984)). As stipulated by one of these principles some of the proposals that we will make here will be guided by the writing tradition that the people already have for their language. It is important to note here that in the course of our research, we requested a number of native speakers to produce some material in writing with the intention of evaluating the writing habits that those who still speak the language have. From these writings we could notice that there was some degree of uniformity in their writing. Of course as we would confirm later as pointed out in Chiatoh (in this volume), there had been an attempt at establishing a literacy programme for the language. Even though it failed, a group of people were already partially literate in the language. It is therefore important to start this discussion with that alphabet. However, this is preceded by an overview of the principles outlined in the 1984 General Alphabet which we will use as yardstick for the orthography that we propose.

7.1 An Overview of the General Principles of Orthography Design for Cameroonian Languages

The following principles are enshrined in the above cited General Alphabet for the design of individual alphabets for Cameroonian indigenous languages.

   i. **Unification of Graphemes**: This principle requires that efforts should be made in representing phonetic sounds in the same way in various languages.
   ii. **Harmonisation of Graphemes**: If for any reason principle (i) cannot hold, then the justification why similar sounds to be presented with different graphemes should be explained.
   iii. **Conventional Perspective**: This principle requires that writing habits already existing and other social factors should be taken into consideration in proposing an alphabet for a language.
   iv. **Practical Utility**: It is important that the proposed alphabet be practical. That is, people should be able to use it in hand writing the language; letters should be found on the key board to facilitate typing and publishing.
   v. **Ease of Reading and Writing:** The graphemes chosen should facilitate reading and writing for the native speaker of the language allowing for no confusion or ambiguity.
   vi. **Preference for Phonemic Representation**: The letters used in writing a language should preferably represent the phonemes of that language. Allophones should only be represented in the alphabet in exceptional circumstances such as social demands.

With these principles, let us now examine the alphabet that was proposed for Nfaw. Given that an alphabet is a graphic representation of the sounds of a language, it is important to begin with a presentation of the phonemes of Nfaw. The phonemes are drawn from Neba (in this volume).

7.2 Nfaw Sounds
7.2.1 Nfaw Phonemic consonant Sounds

Place of Art \ Manner of Art	Bilabial	Labio-velar	Alveolar	Alveo-palatal	Palatal	Velar	Labio-velar	Glottal
Stops	p b		t d			k	kp gb	ʔ
	m		n		ɲ	ŋ	ŋw	
Fricatives		f	s	ʃ				
Affricates		bv		dʒ			kf gv	
Approximants			l		j		w	
Prenasals	ᵐp ᵐb		ⁿt ⁿd			ŋk ŋg		
Implosives	ɓ							

7.2.2 Nfaw Phonemic vowel Sounds

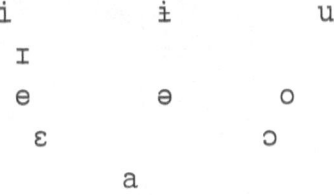

7.2.3 Currently Used Nfaw Orthography
The following letters are found in the Nfaw alphabet proposed by the Bafaw Language Development Committee (1999):

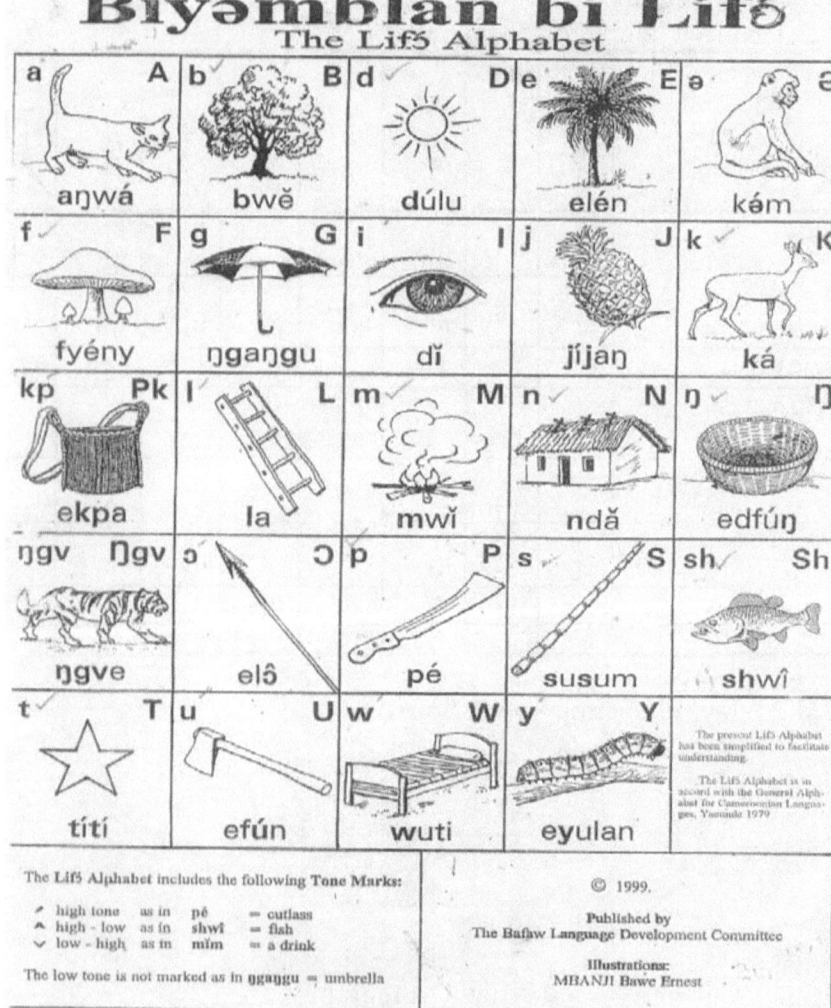

7.3 Discussion

An observation of the chart above reveals that the existing orthography has 27 graphemes: three tones, 6 vowels and 18 consonants. As required by principle vi above, the alphabet is phonemic with all the palatalised, nasalised and labialised sounds excluded. There are a number of sounds which are on the phonemic chart but which do not feature in the said orthography. These are the glottal stop [ʔ], the voiceless bilabial affricate [kf] (even though its voiced counterpart is represented), the labial-velars [kp] and [gb], only one prenasal is represented whereas there exist many more prenasals, and the implosive [ɓ]. As for the vowels, the letter ɔ exists while o does not. This violates principle iv given that the type writer keyboard has the letter o but not ɔ. It will be better to have o in the writing system than have ɔ. This will facilitate utility of the alphabet. [ɨ] is absent from the orthography.

7.4 Our Proposal

Our analysis of the language leads us to the following proposals for the accompanying reasons:

We propose that the grapheme kp should not be included in the alphabet. This is because the letters k and p already exist in the alphabet. The sound [kp] can be captured by using these two letters as a consonant letter cluster. This will not create any problems in writing; rather, it will meet the economy principle. Similarly, the grapheme ŋgv should be eliminated from the writing since g and v exist in the alphabet. We however suggest that g should be included as a grapheme. This letter can also be written as letter clusters. By the way, since the nasal in prenasalised consonants is homorganic, it will be good to replace this consonant with an m before bilabials and n before other consonants. That is, [mb] should be written as mb, [ŋk, ŋg] should be written as nk and ng respectively. In doing this, all the prenasals will be captured and the orthography will be simplified.

We also propose that the sound [ŋ] should be represented in the orthography with ng. In which case, we will not need a grapheme for this sound since n and g already exists as graphemes. However, this proposal poses a difficulty. This will mean that the diagraph ng in the orthography will ambiguously represent [ŋ] and [ŋg]. In other words, how do we read the Nfaw word **ngùshú** -'corn'? Should it be pronounced as [ŋùʃú] or as [ŋgùʃú]? The solution that we propose for this is that at onset position, the grapheme ng should be read as the prenasal [ŋg] and in coda position; it should be read as [ŋ]. Thus the word for 'corn' should be read as [ŋgùʃú].

On the other hand, the diagraph sh representing the sound [ʃ] will need to appear as a grapheme since the grapheme h does not exist in the language[1]. The glottal stop may not be represented since its occurrence in the language is restricted and occurs only optionally in certain positions (clause finally see chapter two). Similarly, the implosive [ɓ] should not be included due to its limitation in occurrence. The sound [ɲ] can be represented in the writing system with a combination of the graphemes n and y. As a result, it does not need to be represented in the alphabet (see also footnote 1).

As far as the vowel sounds are concerned, we propose that ɔ should be replaced with o for ease of writing. The vowel sounds [ɛ], [ɨ] and [ə] should be represented in the writing as [e]. The reason is twofold: aesthetic and ease of representation. In addition, the phonemic distinction apparently lost can easily be recovered in context.

The suggestions that we have made here are motivated by the spontaneous writing activities undertaken by the native speakers who are already trying their hand at it. As indicated in language engineering literature, spontaneous lexification of a language can inform the engineer about the strategies to adopt in expanding the lexicon of a language, (Chumbow and Tamanji 1994). When one examines the way that non- literate native speakers will represent these sounds when writing names and other words, it is glaring that they will easily accept an orthography in which [ɔ] is represented as o, [ɨ] and [ə] are represented as e etc.

With these comments, there are two options that we propose for Bafaw below.

I.   Aa, Bb, Cc, Dd, Ee, Ff, Gg, Ii, Jj, Kk, Ll, Mm, Nn, Oo, Pp, Ss, Hh, Tt, Uu, Vv, Ww, Yy, Zz.

In the first option we have avoided all diagraphs as it is the case with the English language.

II. Aa, Bb, Cc, Dd, Ee, Ff, Gg, Ii, Jj, Kk, KFkf, KPkp, GBgb, Ll, Mm, Nn, NYny, Oo, Pp, Ss, SHsh, Tt, Uu, Vv, Ww, Yy, Zz.

In the second option, we include all the diagraphs. An observation of the two options reveals that the one with diagraphs is more complex than the one without diagraphs. As we have pointed out in footnote 1, since the native speakers are already used to the English writing system, it is likely that they will prefer option one to option two. We make the two options available for any possible experiments in the implementation of the orthography. For the purpose of this work we adopt the first option.

As for the tone marks we adopt those proposed by the Bafaw language committee namely that the High, falling and rising tones should be marked.

We are of the opinion that avoiding the introduction of unnecessary sounds will encourage literacy in the language which will in turn result in the revitalisation of the language.

Notes

1. It is also an option to avoid diagraphs completely by introducing h as one of the graphemes so that the grapheme sh can just be conceived as letter clusters in writing. This will be advantageous because many native speakers are already literate in English and they already have the English tradition of writing. Introducing new sounds may discourage the speakers from making an effort to become literate in the language.

References

Chiatoh, B. A. (In this Volume) Towards the Development of a Functional Bafaw Literacy Programme.

Chumbow, B.S. and P. N. Tamanji, (1994) "Development of Terminology in African Language: Mechanisms of Lexical Expansion". Paper presented at the First Mozambican Workshop on Educational use of African Languages and the Role of LWCS. Maputo, Mozambique, 21 - 23 November 1994.

Neba, A.N. (In this volume) Aspects of the Phonology of Bafaw.

Tadadjeu, Maurice and Etienne Sadembouo. 1979. General alphabet of Cameroon languages. PROPELCA 1. University of Yaounde.

Chapter Eight

Thematic Glossary of Nfaw

Emmanuel Ndzi Tabah and Emmanuel N. Chia

8.0 Introduction

Chumbow (1993) defines a thematic glossary as "an assembly of basic specialised terms in use in a specific domain or field of knowledge... in order to facilitate the communication of knowledge available in the international community to a linguistic community that does not have that knowledge". The development of thematic glossaries for indigenous African languages is particularly important given the link between such specialised knowledge and national development. Chumbow (1985) holds that many attempts at mass literacy have been futile in Africa because they were carried out in an exoglossic language. Accordingly, for technical/specialised knowledge (especially in fields which are of immediate importance to the masses) to be disseminated effectively, there is need for basic specialised vocabulary to be developed.

In this chapter, we seek to address the question of expressing new knowledge in Nfaw. It is certain that we cannot possibly establish exhaustive thematic glossaries for all the themes in a document of this nature. As a result, we intend to focus the identification of the different strategies that can be used for a massive lexical expansion in Nfaw. We do hope that once this is done, the processes can then be applied by others in the development of different thematic glossaries. In our current work, we will limit our examples in three areas: agriculture, health care delivery, and religion.

8.1 Methodology

In order to identify the different processes that can be used for the development of thematic glossaries in Nfaw, a number of words (the SIL comparative word list) were elicited from native speakers. The words were then analysed to discover how those concepts were named. In cases where borrowing was done we studied those words to see if the borrowed words were adapted and how. The analysis was inspired by the structural analysis already done in previous chapters of this volume. Where there was coinage, we determined how they were coined; whether it was motivated by description, onomatopoeia, etc. After identifying and describing the different strategies of spontaneous nomenclature in the language, we then evaluated by counting the number of words which were either coined or loan adapted to determine the extent to which each mechanism was used. Our expectation was that given the situation of the language and with many of the few speakers, mainly literate in the English language, loan adaptation was going to be dominantly used. Contrary to this hypothesis, it was overwhelmingly clear that many of the speakers still relied on coinage as a strategy of naming in the language. The results of this research are presented in the sections that follow and examples of thematic glossaries are given in the end of the chapter.

8.2 Mechanisms of Lexical Expansion Spontaneously used in Bafaw

A number of mechanisms have been identified as common strategies used by African languages for naming concepts (Chumbow and Tamanji 1994, Mutaka and Tamanji 2004). These are coinage, borrowing and semantic extension. It has also been established that coinage is the most natural and most preferred with semantic extension second and borrowing the third. However, in some languages, it has been noticed that while a majority of the older population and those illiterate in English and French will prefer coinage, the younger population employ borrowing, sometimes with very little adaptation. We consider the case of Nfaw below.

8.2.1 Coinage
By coinage we mean that the language meets a new concept from another language/culture, but uses its own resources to name the concept. As Numfor (1999) puts it, "language A" borrows a new concept from "language B" but the resources of "language A" are used in referring to the concept. For example: **ndébàsì** 'church', **ndéŋkùlù** 'hospital'. The concepts of 'hospital' and 'church' are

borrowed concepts and spontaneously new referents have been assigned to them using the resources of the language. The word for 'church' is formed from **ndá** 'house' and **èbàsì** 'a cross coastal narrow Bantu word for god, religious organisation'. The word literally means 'god's house'. The word for 'hospital' is derived in a similar way. Again it comes from the word for 'house' and **éŋkfùlù** 'sickness' which literally means, 'a house for sicknesses. It is important to note that the rule of vowel deletion discussed in chapter two applies deleting one of two contiguous vowels across morphemes.

Coinage can be achieved through a number of strategies namely,

A. **Description/Function:** In Nfaw, names are given to some concepts based on how the concepts look or where they are located and how they function for example; **èkpútú** which literally means the 'cap of a house'. This name is a description of the way the roof seats on a house, like a cap on one's head. The house is conceived as wearing a cap which is the roof. Unlike in many other Bantu languages in Cameroon which generally name a roof as the 'head of a house' when they coin, Nfaw uses 'cap of a house'. This is a motivation for the study of the structure of individual languages in the process of lexical expansion. Even though there may be general tendencies that cut across many related languages as have been demonstrated in the literature, many languages still reserve a number of idiosyncratic features that require careful study so as to avoid rejection because of artificiality.

B. **Semantic Extension:** This is a very widely used strategy in Nfaw like in many other African languages. By semantic extension is meant that a language borrows a new concept but extends the meaning of an existing word in the language to cover this new concept. Sometimes this is accompanied by some amount of modification to distinguish the new concept from the existing one. For example:

8.2.2 Borrowing

Borrowing refers to a situation whereby language A borrows a concept from language B together with its name. In such a situation, the borrowed name has to be adapted to suit the natural structure (syllable structure, morpheme structure, word structure, etc.) of the language. Neba, Chumbow and Tamanji (2006) have summarised some of the loan adaptation strategies employed across the board in African languages. In this section of the chapter, we examine some of the loan adaptation strategies that are used spontaneously in Nfaw and which can be exploited for lexical expansion for the language. Generally, Nfaw borrows from French, English, Pidgin English and a host of other African languages. However, given that there are no significant adaptations of words borrowed from other African languages and to a large extent, Pidgin English, we concentrated on the adaptation of words borrowed from English and French whose structures are markedly different from that of Nfaw. The usual processes of cluster simplification, dediphthongisation, and etc.

These various mechanisms have been used to develop the Nfaw items that we present below. At the entry for 'condom' for example, the Nfaw equivalent is mànyóngò. This is the word for "rubber" in this language. Thus by semantic extension, this word takes on the meaning of condom, since condoms are made from rubber. Where the Nfaw words are borrowed the items have been shaped to respect the morpheme structure conditions of the language. The Nfaw word for hospital for example, is wàspíta. The *tl* cluster at the end of the word has been simplified to *ta* while the *h* has been changed to *w*. Similarly, abstract nouns like *protein* and *vitamin* have been assigned a nominal class indicated by the nasal that is prefixed to each- *mprónte* and *nvitamin* respectively. Finally, many of the words have been developed by a combination of more than one mechanism of lexical expansion. The Nfaw term for "antibody" in this glossary for example, is *anti nyàmbέ*. Thus, only the prefix, anti- is borrowed and used with a Nfaw word, *nyàmbέ* (disease). The word for *antigen* is then developed from this by description: nyàmú àntí nyámbέ (something that produces àntí nyámbɛ). It is note worthy at this point that both of our informants[1] consistently demonstrated a preference for indigenous words over borrowed items such that we only turned to borrowing as a last resort. Consequently, many of the Nfaw terms have been developed by description. The Nfaw word for tuberculosis, for example, is *èkwésiégbi* which means "bad cough".

8.3 Organisation of the glossary

The terms in this glossary are organised under three themes: agriculture, health care delivery, and religion. The entries under each theme have been presented in alphabetical order for easy reference. For each term, we provide the Nfaw equivalent followed by the part of speech, a simple definition in English, and an example of its use in a sentence in Nfaw (with the gloss in English).

8.3.1 Nfaw Thematic Glossary
8.3.1.1 Agriculture
In a country where 75% of the population is involved in agriculture either for subsistence or as an income earner, it is necessary to develop terms in indigenous languages so that useful information on aspects such as new farming methods, pest control, crop protection and food preservation can be easily disseminated. This section presents selected terms in agriculture.

Aerial root: *mbùkà ɛ mìnyǝ* [N] Roots which hang from above ground portion of a plant without reaching the ground. Ex. à dí túm á *mbùkà ɛ mìnyǝɹ* "*It is difficult to walk on aerial roots*"

Bush fallowing: *nfálò ndùkú* [N] Not cultivating crops on a piece of land so that it might regain fertility
Ex.
ndʒi ndùkú émé die élólí bwĕ *nfálò nd ùkú*.
'When a farm is old, it is good to practice bush fallowing.'

Cabbage: *kábèdʒi* [N] Kinds of cultivated plant with thick leaves and a round head, cooked as a vegetable.
Ex. élólí diáʔ *kábèdʒi*
'It is good to eat cabbages.'

Carrots: *károt* [N] Orange-red root, used as a vegetable.
Ex. *károt ébĕ vitamin*.
'Carrots give vitamins.'

Cash crop: *mue é ŋga* [N] Crop grown for selling rather than for use as food.
Ex. kàkáò édí *mue é ŋga* 'Cocoa is a cash crop.'

Chlorophyll: *klorofil* [N] Green substance in plants that absorbs light to help them grow.
Ex. biĕ bíwoŋi *klorofil* 'Leaves contain chlorophyll.'

Compost manure: *mànyú a ébùka* [N] Manure formed from decayed matter.
Ex. *mànyú a ébùka élólí túmbí fètàl áisa* 'Compost manure is better than fertilizer.'

Cotton: *kotin* [N] Crop grown in warm areas for the soft white hairs around its seed used in making thread.
Ex. bá bwĕ mìkù nà *kotin* 'They make clothes with cotton.'

Cover crop: *èshùm ékùti* [N] Crop planted to prevent the soil from being washed away.
Ex. *élólí ádi wùn èshùm ékùtia ndùkú màn yóngo* 'It is good to plant cover crops in rubber farms.'

Crop rotation: *ndùkú ə́ rùteshon* [N] Alternating the crops that are cultivated on a piece of land to prevent it from being impoverished.
ndùkú ə́ rùteshon ə́pànan mànyu. 'Crop rotation brings fertility.'

Dairy farming: *ndùkú ə́ dárì* [N] Rearing animals for the production of milk. Ex. *ndùkú ə́ dárɪ ə́ bə̌ mílíkì.* 'Dairy farming produces milk.'

Fertilizer: *fetalaisa* [N] Chemical plant food.
Ex. *mànyú a ébùka élólí túmbí fètàláisa*' Compost manure is better than fertilizer.'

Fodder plant: *dediáʔ də nyà* [N] Plant that is grown to serve as food for horses and farm animals.
Ex. *ediáʔ də nyà ékámbi á adiwòŋ* 'Fodder is not difficult to have.'

Food crop: *mùe édídia* [N] Crop that is grown for food rather than to be sold.
Ex.
mùe édídia ewoŋì a ŋgá ŋgə̀ muə ŋgà 'Food crops do not fetch money like cash crops.

Forestry: *lìwúkú défin* [N] The practice of planting and taking care of forests.
Ex.
bábáne ɲǐa ádə́ wuku lìwúkú défin 'people don't like to study forestry.'

Garden: *gádìn* [N] Piece of land around a house where flowers, fruits, vegetables, etc can be grown.
Ex.
élólí ádə́ wún yàmbayámba a gádin. 'It is good to plant vegetables in a garden.'

Herbicide: *bwèbí bìshùm* [N] Chemical that kills herbs.
Ex.
bwèbí bìshùm bíbulu bìshùn á ndùkú 'Herbicides kill weeds in the farm.'

Infertile soil: *ndò è bîi* [N] Soil that cannot produce good crops.
Ex.
màdía má sə bwĕ bwam á ndò è bîi. 'crops don't do well in infertile soil.'

Irrigation: *bè ndŏo mádi* [N] The practice of supplying water to a piece of land through pipes and channels so that crops can grow.
Ex.
bá sĕ bwèlá bè ndŏo mádi a púndə èmbŭ 'We don't do irrigation during the rainy season.'

Mixed cropping: *ndùkú ə́ miks* [N] The practice of growing several types of crops together.
Ex.
ndùkú ə́ miks ébé màdi nyài na nyài. mixed cropping produce different crops.'

Nursery: *nósəri* [N] A place where young plants and trees are grown for planting elsewhere.
Ex. *ádé bwĕ nósəri kàkáò élólí.* 'It is good to make a cocoa nursery.'

Pasture: *bìshùm* [N] Land covered with grass that is suitable for feeding animals on.
a púndə mbú bìshùm bíba dʒità. 'During the rainy season there is a lot of pasture.'

Pest: *bìkàkáŋ bíbi* [N] An insect or animal that destroys plants, food etc.
Ex.
bìkàkáŋ bíbi bilúŋgú bă a ndùkú ə kàkáò. 'pests are usually found in cocoa farms.'

Pesticide: mbùlà bìkàkáŋ [N] Chemical used in killing pests.
Ex.
ndʒi ébwèláni mbùlà bìkàkáŋ á ndùkú k àkáò ébulu bəbibi
'when we use pesticides on a farm they kill pests.'

Pollen grains: polin [N] Fine powder that is produced by a flower and carried to other flowers of the same type to enable them produce fruit.
Ex.
ndùkú ŋkui élúŋgu wǒŋ polin à ŋgondì ébê. 'A maize farm produces pollen after two months.'

Poultry: ndáèkfú [N] Chickens, duck and geese kept for their meat. Ex. ndáèkfu ékámbìáʔ ádiluŋ. 'A poultry farm is not difficult to build.'

Ranch: wùkâ bú nyà [N] Large farm where cows, horses, sheep etc are breed.
Ex.
wùkâ bú nyà bi di dʒità á bamenda. 'There are many cattle ranches in Bamenda.'

Soil conservation: kòŋgó ndo [N] Preventing the soil from being destroyed.
Ex.
fama tə alòlí bǐ a di kòŋgó ndo. 'Every farmer should know how to practice soil conservation.'

Subsistence agriculture: ndùkú sòbsistèn [N] Growing crops mainly for food not to be sold.
Ex.
ndùkú sòbsistèn éwóŋìáʔ ŋgà. 'Subsistence farming does not bring money.'

Taproot: ŋkàŋgá nnên [N] Root that grows deep into the ground.
Ex. bwě dʒità bí wóŋi ŋkàŋgá nnên. 'Most trees have tap roots.'

Topsoil: ndò èmínye [N] The layer of soil that is nearest the surface of the ground.
Ex.
ndò èmínye dódí wúŋgû wóɲi mànyú. 'The top soil is usually fertile.'

Transpiration: èdí ébie [N] Loss of water by plants through their leaves.
Ex.   èdí ébie élóliáʔ dʒità. 'Excessive transpiration is not good.'

Transplant: trànsiplànté [V] Move a growing plant and pant it somewhere.
Ex.
élólí adé trànsiplànté a púndə mbŭ. 'It's good to transplant during the rainy season.'

Water conservation: kòŋgó màdi [N] Preventing water resources from being destroyed, e.g., by planting forests around water sources.
Ex.
ádí wun bwĕ a fùmbú màdi édí bwam adi kòŋgó màdi
'Planting trees around water sources is good for water conservation.'

Water table: tébelì a màdi [N] The level at which water is found in the ground.
Ex.
púndə émbù tébelì a màdi é ba emĭ. 'During the rainy season the water table is usually high.'

Watering can: kân a màdi. [N] A metal container in which water is put for watering crops.
Ex.
kân a màdi élólí ádí bwèlàn à noseri.
'A watering can is good for use in a nursery.'

8.3.1.2 Health Care Delivery

AIDS: nyàmbéwàm [N] Acquired immune deficiency syndrome. A disease which makes the body incapable of resisting infection. nyàmbéwàm édi nyàmbé ebǐ
'Aids is a dangerous disease.'

Antibody: àntɪ nyàmbé [N] Chemical substance specifically produced by the body in response to invasion.
Ex. nyàmbéwàm ebúlú àntɪ nyàmbɛ́. 'Aids kills antibodies.'

Antigen: nyàmú ànti nyàmbɛ́ [N] A substance which stimulates the formation of antibodies.
Ex.
nyàmú ànti nyàmbɛ́ dʒódi yě antinyàmbé.
'Antigens produce antibodies.'

Bacteria: mbàktiria [N] A large group of unicellular and multicellular organisms lacking chlorophyll that cause infections.
mbàktiria dʒódi pànán bà nyàmbé
'Bacteria cause diseases.'

Balanced diet: dìdiá dímba [N] The right quantity and variety of food necessary for good health.
Ex.
dìdiá dímba di lólí nà mwàlân na wùtû
'A balanced diet is good for a pregnant woman.'

Birth control: kòntərol é diyá [N] The practice of controlling the number of children one has using various methods of contraception. kòntərol é diyá élólí
'Birth control is good.'

Blood circulation: ɛ̀kě máki [N] The movement of blood around the body.
Ex.
ɛ̀kě máki dódí bwě mò à bá lùŋgé. 'Blood circulation keeps people alive.'

Blood group: nyà ə̀ màki [N] Any of the different types into which human blood is separated.
Ex. élólí a di bí nyà ə̀ màki ə wə̀. 'It is good to know your blood group.'

Blood pressure: preshò imàki [N] The pressure of blood as it travels around the body.
Ex.
ndʒí ə kìyé waspita bá lúŋgú nùŋ pres ho ə màkí
'When you go to the hospital they usually take your blood pressure.'

Cancer: kánsa [N] Serious disease in which there is an abnormal growth of cells which eventually kill the normal body cells.
Ex. kánsa ébulu bă dʒítà. 'Cancer kills many people.'

Child birth: dìya [N] (See birth control).

Cholera: nyàmbé kólirà [N] A water borne disease which causes severe diarrhoea and vomiting.
Ex.
ndʒi ə mwili màdí èmbùndù etíŋgání wŏ ŋnyàmbé
kólirà 'If you drink dirty water you can catch cholera.'

Conception: lèwóŋwótò [N] The process of an egg being fertilized inside a woman so that she becomes pregnant.
lèwóŋwótò édi ámákè ma duə. 'Conception is the work of God.'

Condom: mànyóngò [N] A thin rubber covering that a man wears over his penis to prevent a woman from getting pregnant or to protect against disease.

Ex.
élólí a dí bwèlán mànyóngò ndʒi esákì á adé won nyàmbé wàm. 'It is good to use a condom if you don't want to catch Aids.'

Conjunctivitis: àpòlò. [N] An infectious eye disease that causes pain and swelling in part of the eye
Ex. àpòlò édí nyàmbé dĭs. 'Conjunctivitis is an eye disease.'

Constipation: èkúpa [N] The condition of being unable to get rid of waste matter from the bowels easily.
Ex.
ndì èdílí dʒítà ètíŋgání wŏŋ èkúpá 'When you eat too much you will suffer from constipation.'

Contraception: kontərasépshòn [N] The practice of preventing a woman from getting pregnant.
Ex.
bá bwèlán kontərasépshòn à də kòntəro lé dìya. 'We use contraception for birth control.'

Contraceptive: bwèbútátì wùtû [N] Any drug, device, or practice that prevents a woman from getting pregnant.

Convulsion: énó [N] A sudden shaking movement of the body that can not be controlled.
Ex. énó élúŋgú walé băn. 'Convulsion is common in children'

Dandruff: bìfá [N] Very small pieces of dead skin, seen as white dust in a person's hair.
Ex. bìfá édi nyàmbé nyŏo. 'Dandruff is a skin disease'

Dehydration: dihaidəreshon [N] The process in which a person loses too much water from the body.

Ex.

ewóŋé nyàmbé kólirà éwòŋ dihaidəreshon.
'When you have cholera you suffer dehydration.'

Diabetes: nyàmbê a shúkà [N] Medical condition in which there is excessive sugar in the blood.

Ex.

ndʒĭ ewoni nyàmbê a shúkà etíŋgáni wo ŋ nlĕm ŋkúndi. 'When you have diabetes you can easily have heart failure.'

Digestion: lìbùm lípiéti [N] The process in which food is changed into substances which the body can absorb.
Ex. ndʒĭ emuli músáló etíngání wŏŋ lìbùm lípiéti. 'If you suck oranges it eases digestion.'

Digestive tract: bùkàn dìdiá [N] System of organs in the body through which food passes and which function in digestion.
Ex. dìdía di tum a bùkàn dìdiá. 'Food passes through the digestive tract.'

Dizziness: mìmálífín [N] Condition in which people feel that everything is spinning.

Ex.

ndʒĭ a wóŋì á màki dʒìta etíŋgáni wŏ ŋ mìmálífín. 'If you don't have enough blood you experience dizziness.'

Drunkenness: wùmwámwâ [N] State of being drunk or having taken too much alcohol.

Ex.

wùmwámwa élólíáʔ na mò wo a kànàn èkí.
'Drunkenness is not good for a driver.'

Dwarfism: *éshùpúndʒì* [N] Condition in which people are very short, with short arms and legs.
Ex.
éshùpúndʒì eshǐaʔ a wúfaw étin. 'Dwarfism is not common among the Bafaw.'

Ebola fever: *ìŋkfùlù èbòlà* [N] Fever caused by Ebola virus.
Ex.
ìŋkfùlù èbòla edí nyàmbé ŋkóne. 'Ebola fever is a new disease.'

Ebola virus: *èbòlà* [N] Virus that causes Ebola fever. Ex. *èbòlà* diodi bwě *ìŋkfùlù èbòlà*.

First aid: *lìwúndʒáŋ díwúso* [N] Simple medical treatment that is given to someone before the doctor arrives or before the person is taken to the hospital.
Ex.
ndʒǐ ewóŋé áksidèn *lìwúndʒáŋ díwúso* dí yumimbǎ. 'When you have an accident first aid is very important.'

Gastritis: *gástirìk* [N] An illness caused by inflammation of the epithelium lining the stomach.
Ex.
gástirìk e bi nyàmbé mbùkàn dìdia 'Gastritis is a disease of the digestive tract.'

Gonorrhoea: *nyàmbé á mànya* [N] A disease that affects the sexual organs caused by having sex with an infected person.
Ex.
ndʒǐ èbwèlani mànyóŋgò etingani wǒŋ n yàmbé á mànya. 'If you use a condom you can't catch gonorrhoea.'

Heart Disease : *nyàmbê a nlěm* [N]

Heart failure: nlĕm ŋkúndi [N] Serious condition in which the heart does not work properly.
Ex.
ndʒĭ ewoni nyàmbê a shúkà etíŋgáni wo ŋ nlĕm ŋkúndi. 'When you have diabetes you can easily have heart failure.

HIV: echaivi Human immune virus- the virus that causes Aids.
Ex. echaivi diódí pànăn nyàmbéwàm. 'HIV causes Aids.'

Indigestion: èkúpa [N] *(see constipation)*

Laxative: èsùŋ [N] Any substance that causes people to empty their bowels easily.
Ex. bá **bwèlán èsùn ádí wa dìbùm.** 'We use laxatives to cleanse the bowels.'

Malaria: ŋgŏŋkèlè [N] Disease that causes shivering and fever, caused by the bite of some types of mosquito.
Ex. mòskitò diódì bĕ ŋgŏŋkèlè. 'Mosquitoes cause malaria.'

Menses: ŋgòn [N] The flow of blood each month from a woman's body.
Ex.
bàlân bá **lúŋgú wŏn màkí ma ŋgòn.** 'Women usually have their menses monthly.'

Midwife: ŋkuámwan [N] Person (especially a woman) who is trained to help women give deliver.
ŋkuámwan a bwĕ ebùlù a màtániti. 'A midwife works in a maternity.'

Nutrient: nyútrèn [N] A substance that is needed by living things for growth and energy.
Ex. mà dia má wóŋí nyútren. 'Food contains nutrients.'

Placenta: ɛ̀sán [N] Material that comes out of a woman or female animal after a child has been born.
Ex.
ndʒǐ nwalán a mə yé ba lólí wùshí èsá n ə
mwan. 'When a woman delivers we have to bury the placenta.'

Poliomyelitis: lìbiéŋ. [N] A disease that affects the central nervous system and can cause temporal or permanent paralysis.
bá lólí bébăn mùkélé mú lìbién.
'We have to give children vaccination against polio.'

Proteins: mprɔ́ntè [N] Natural substance found in foods like meat, beans, eggs, etc which is needed by humans and animals for growth. Ex. nyàm nà màkĕ má bĕ **mprɔ́ntè**. 'Meat and eggs give proteins.'

Rehydration: rihaidəreshon [N] The process of restoring water to the body of someone who suffers from dehydration.

Skin disease: nyàmbê a nyŏo [N]
Ex. bìfá édi nyàmbê a nyŏo. 'Dandruff is a skin disease'

Tuberculosis: ɛ̀kwɛ́siégbì [N] Serious infectious disease which causes swellings in the lungs and other parts of the body.
Ex.
bàwó ba wóɲí nyàmbéwàm ba **lúŋgú wóŋ ɛ̀ kwɛ́siégbì**. 'People who have Aids easily catch TB.'

Typhoid: taifod [N] Serious infectious disease which causes fever and severe pain in the bowels.

ètìŋgání wŏŋ táifod á madia ma mbìndù.'
you can catch typhoid from dirty food.'

Vaccination: *mùkélé* [N] Process of giving a protective dose against a disease.
Ex. bá lólí bébăn mùkélé mú lìbién. 'We have to give children vaccination against polio.'

Venereal disease: *nyàmbê a màdúka* [N] Disease that is acquired/spread through sex.
ndʒĭ èbwèlání mànyóngò ètíngànì wŏŋ n yàmbê a màdúka. 'If you use condoms you cannot catch a venereal disease.'

Virus: *vairos* [N] Microscopic organism that causes infections. Ex. echaivi è dí vairos. 'HIV is a virus.'

Vitamin: *nvitamin* [N] Natural substance in food that helps humans and animals grow and stay healthy.
Ex. yàmbayámbá díbĕ nvitamin. 'Vegetables give vitamins'

Ward: *tùŋgéwàspíta* [N] A room in a hospital for patients who have been admitted.
mòwə àwóɲí ŋkfùlù ə nén ba bómé tùŋgé wàspita □'Someone who is seriously sick is admitted in a hospital ward.'

8.3.1.3 Religion
Religion constitutes an integral part of a people's culture. It is therefore necessary to include terms which represent religious concepts in this glossary. Given the widespread influence of Christianity, many of the items under this theme refer to Christian concepts.

Abraham: *Abiraham* [N] Father of the Israeli nation. *Abiraham mó adí samu bă*
ısrael. 'Abraham is the father of the Israelites.'

Adultery: *adótirì* [N] Sex between a married person and someone who is not his or her wife or husband. *adótirì dí nsàm əbìŋ.* 'Adultery is evil.'

Almighty: *duə líŋ mínyéu* [N] Having complete power. Used to refer to God. *duə líŋ mínyéu mɔ á tàtí sə.* 'The All Mighty is the one who takes care of all of us.'

Alpha and Omega: *dèbútí nà dèshúkàn* [N] The beginning and the end. Used to refer to God. *duə mɔ à dí dèbútí nà dèshúkàn.* 'God is the alpha and the omega.

Altar: *ótà* [N] Holy table in a church or temple. *ba bə̆ màsákàn a ótà.* 'We place our offerings on the altar.'

Apostle: *bàwútú ə yesu* [N] Any of the twelve men Christ chose to work with him while on earth. *bá bílé dium nà abê bàwútú ə yesu.* 'There were twelve apostles.'

Ascension: *asenshon* [N] The movement of Christ to Heaven Body and Soul. The day Christ is believed to have gone to heaven in this way. *yesù aŋkə̆ á mǐn a bwìmbú asenshon.* 'Jesus went to heaven on ascension day.'

Backsliding: *tìmbìmbǐ* [N] A situation in which a believer comes back to live a sinful life as he/she lived before becoming a believer. *ndʒǐ wə̀ tìmbìmbǐ a fə mbú ébàsɩ batingani we nunpə.* 'If you backslide from church you can be readmitted.'

Baptize: *námsə* [V] To put a few drops of water on someone or immerse him/her as a sign that the person ha been accepted in a Christian church. *ndǐ èdúbé a yesu* bǎ námsə wê. 'If you believe in Christ you will be baptized.'

Beelzebub: *Satan* [N] Another name for the Devil; Satan. satan a sèɲí Eve. 'Satan deceived Eve.'

Benediction: *benedikshon* [N] A Christian prayer of blessing.
pasitɔ mé a bǎ *benedikshon* a ndǎ ébàs 1. 'The pastor is the one who gives the benediction in church.'

Bible: *kâtè e due* [N] Holy book of the Christian religion made up of 66 books.
mɔ̀ té a lɔ̀lí láŋ *kâtè e due*. 'Everyone should read the Bible.'

Catholic: *pàtà* [N] The main Christian denomination from which other denominations (known as protestants) broke away. The Catholic church has its headquarters in Rome.
ébàsɪèbàsì ə *pàtà* yó bílí èbàsè ewusu.
'The catholic church was the first church.'

Choir: *èlóŋgi* [N] Group of singers especially in a church, who make music during worship.
épàsi tə ewɔɲi *èlóŋgi* emɔ̀. 'Every church has a choir'

Christian: *kristen* [N] A follower of Christ; one who practices the teachings of Jesus Christ.
bà *kristen* bá sǎ dʒǐp. 'Christians should not steal.'

Christianity: *ɛpìpá ə yesu* [N] Religion which follows the teachings of Jesus Christ. *ɛpìpá ə yesu* élɔ́lí. 'Christianity is good.'

Christmas: *ŋgàndì mbú* [N] The day on which Christians commemorate the birth of Christ (25th December).

bá yé ʏesu a bwìmbú ŋgàndì mbú. 'Jesus was born on Christmas.'

Church: ébàsɪ [N] A building where Christians go to worship; a group of Christians who worship together. ébàsɪ tə ewɔɲi èlóŋgi emò. 'Every church has a choir'

Congregation: baà ébàsɪ [N] A group of worshippers; a church. pasitɔ mɔ̀ à dí nlŭ mú baà ébàsɪ. 'The pastor is the head of a congregation.'

Covenant: kóvenàn [N] An agreement especially between God and his people. due àŋwɔŋ kóvenàn à bă ɪsrael. 'God made a covenant with Israel'

Covetousness: èshêe [N] Sin of desiring what belongs to other people. èshêe élólìá? 'Covetousness is not good.'

Crucify: búlú a mbàsa [V] Kill someone by nailing to a wooden bar. Jesus Christ was crucified. bá búlú ʏesu á mbàsa. 'Jesus was crucified.'

Deacon (Deaconess) dikin [N] A religious leader who assists the priest or pastor in the church. In some churches the deacon is not of the clergy. dikin mó á wundʒán pasito á ndə̀ ébàsì. 'A deacon helps the pastor in church.'

Doctrine: wúkù doktrin. [N] The teachings of a religious group. bǎn ba lólí wúkù doktrin ébàsè. 'Children should attend doctrine classes.'

Elder: mùtùlèdi [N] An official in some churches playing similar functions like a deacon.

bamùtùlèdi bóba bɛ̆ dálásango á ba kri sten. 'The elders are those who give communion to Christians.'

Epistle: kâtè epistel [N] Any of the letters written by the first believers that constitute part of the New Testament of the Bible. Paul à tìlì kâtè epistel dʒità. 'Paul wrote many epistles.'

Eternal Life: lòŋgé èsésên. [N] Life that lasts for ever.
bà wó ba dúbé a duə bá wóɲí lòŋgé èsésên. 'Those who believe in God have eternal life.'

Excommunicate: èskominiketi To expel someone from the church, especially the catholic church.
ébàsì è pàtà étíngánê èskominiketi kristen émò. 'The catholic church can excommunicate its members.'

Faith: èdúbe Complete trust in God.
bà wó ba dúbé a duə bá wóɲí lòŋgé èsésên. 'Those who have faith (believe) in God have eternal life.'

Fast: dʒè á duə [N] A period during which people do not eat food for religious reasons.
àdé ba a ndʒè a duə elólí á bàkristen. 'Fasting is good for Christians.'

Good Friday: Friday è mbâa [N] The day Christ is believed to have been crucified.
Yesu a wílí a friday ə mbâa. 'Jesus died on Good Friday.'

Good Samaritan: samaritaa é mbǎa [N] The Samaritan in one of Jesus' parables who took care of a Jewish stranger.
samaritan é mbǎa mɔ̀ a mbùkánʒè. 'The good Samaritan helped someone on the way.'

Gospel: ŋkàlàn dùə [N] The good news about Christ.

bà kristen ba lólí lòŋbâ ŋkàlàn dùə.
'Christians should preach the Gospel.'

Hell: *hêl* [N] The place believed to be home of devils where evil people go after death.
bà wɔ́ ba dúbèá? duə ba lólí kĕ á *hêl*

Immortal: *àsĕwă* [Adj.] That cannot die. duə *àsĕwă*. 'God is immortal'

Islam: *ɪsilàm* [N] Religion practised by followers of Mohamed.
ɪsilàm edi èdúbe é ŋgvùsà. 'Islam is the religion of Muslims.'

Koran: *Kuran* [N] Holy book of Muslims.
kuran edí kâte duə a ba ŋgvùsà. 'The Koran is the holy book of Muslims.'

Muslim: *ŋgvùsà* [N] Follower of Mohamed; one who practices Islam. *ɪsilàm edi èdúbe é ŋgvùsà*. 'Islam is the religion of Muslims.'

Pagan: *pégèn*. [N] A person who does not follow the religious beliefs of any of the world's major religions.
bà pégèn bá dúbèá? duə. 'Pagans don't believe in God.'

Parable: *panabul* [N] A short story that teaches a moral or spiritual lesson. yesu a nlùfú bâ nà panabul. 'Jesus taught people using parables.'

Paradise: *á mìnyə* [N] Heaven; perfect place where people go when they die.
bá wɔ bá dúbé duə ba kĕ mìnyə ndʒí bá wílí. 'Those who believe in God will go to heaven when they die.'

Passover: *túmbà mínyə* [N] The Jewish religious feast in commemoration of their escape from Egypt.

Pastor: *pásíto* [N] Spiritual leader of some Christian churches.
dikin mɔ́ á wundʒán

pasito á ndə́ ébàsì. 'A deacon helps the pastor in church.'

Sin: *wùbî* An offence against God.

Soul: *nləm wútìtîn* [N] The spiritual part of a person which lives on after the body dies.

mɔ̀ te a wóɲí nləm wútìtîn. 'Every human being has a soul.'

The Ten Commandments: *mbía dium é duə* [N] Ten laws given by God to the Israelites through their leader, Moses.

bà kristen bá lólí kòŋgǒ mbía diu é d uə 'Christians should keep the ten commandments.'

Vision: *nlúʔméyo* [N] A dream in which one has a revelation from God, angels, etc.

Notes

1. Mr Eeme Maurice Mwele, and ... University of Buea

References

Chumbow, B.S 1993. "Thematic Glossaries and Language Development" Paper presented at LAUD Symposium in Duisburg, Germany.

Collocott, and Dobson, A. B (eds) 1974. *Chambers Science and Technology Dictionary*. Chamber Ltd

Cook, A. J 1978. *A B C of Plant Terms* Merrow Publishing Co Ltd

www.ingramcontent.com/pod-product-compliance
Lightning Source LLC
Chambersburg PA
CBHW021407290426
44108CB00010B/420